The Imitation of Christ

In Four Books

The Imitation of Christ

In Four Books

by

Thomas à Kempis

A New Translation from the Original Latin

by

Joseph N. Tylenda, S.J.

Michael Glazier, Inc.
Wilmington, Delaware

ABOUT THE TRANSLATOR

Joseph N. Tylenda, S.J., is Managing Editor and Book Review Editor of *Theological Studies* magazine. He is a member of the Georgetown University Jesuit Community and has recently completed *Portraits in American Sanctity* (1983), and *Jesuit Saints and Martyrs* (1984).

Published in 1984 by MICHAEL GLAZIER, INC., 1723 Delaware Avenue, Wilmington, Delaware 19806 ● ● Library of Congress Catalog Card Number: 84-80349 ● International Standard Book Number: 0-89453-432-7 (Michael Glazier, Inc.) ● Cover design by Lillian Brulc ● Typography by Joyce Cartagena ● Printed in the United States of America.

To E. J. A.
who loves God and desires to
walk in the footsteps of Jesus
His only Son

CONTENTS

Book II

Directives for the Interior Life

Book III

On Interior Consolation

Book IV

On the Blessed Sacrament

INTRODUCTION

The Imitation of Christ is the most famous and most beloved Christian devotional book ever written, and its popularity today equals the popularity it enjoyed when it was first composed. By 1471, the year of Thomas à Kempis' death, the book had been so frequently hand copied and passed to monastery after monastery that there are extant today some 700 manuscripts of this medieval classic. With the invention of printing *The Imitation* enjoyed still greater favor; its first printed edition appeared in Augsburg in 1471/1472, and in the ensuing 500 years it has gone through innumerable editions. Some 1800 of them had been catalogued in 1779; today, in the mid-1980s, this number is beyond computation. In addition, the book has been translated into more than 50 languages, and in English alone there are some 60 names associated with this masterpiece, either as translator or revisor/adaptor of an earlier translation.

The Imitation has been the favorite reading of philosophers and poets, saints and statesmen. St. Thomas More (1478-1535), England's Lord Chancellor under Henry VIII, listed it as one of the three books that should find their way into everyone's hands, and St. Ignatius of Loyola (1491-1556), who read a chapter each day of his life, was in the habit of offering it as a gift to acquaintances. St. Robert Bellarmine (1542-1621), Cardinal of the Roman Church, repeatedly returned to it and no matter how often he read it, he always found new fruit. The German philosopher Gottfried Wilhelm von Leibniz (1646-1716) considered *The Imitation* to be the most excellent treatise ever written, and John Wesley (1703-1791), founder of Methodism, judged it to be the best summary of the Christian life and translated it for his followers. Pierre Corneille (1606-1684), France's greatest dramatist, put its noble thoughts into verse, and Ireland's patriot Daniel O'Connell (1775-1847) used it for daily meditation. Thomas Merton (1915-1968), America's most popular ascetical writer, acknowledged that *The Imitation* was one of the first rays of light that led to his conversion, and Pope John Paul I (1912-1978) was reading the book when death unexpectedly called him on the night of September 28, 1978, after only 33 short days as Roman Pontiff.

Authorship

Since the earliest manuscripts of *The Imitation* are anonymous, the work has over the years been attributed to a variety of ecclesiastical authors. Some 25 names have been advanced, and among them we find: St. Augustine (354-430), St. Anselm (1033-1109), St. Bernard (1091-1153), Giovanni Gersen (+ about 1243), St. Bonaventure (1221-1274), Jean Gerson (1363-1429), and Thomas à Kempis (1380-1471). That the book should first appear anonymously is not surprising since the author advocates in Book I, chap. 2, that we should "love to be unknown." In 1434, when John de Bellerive presented a manuscript copy of the book to the Brethren of the Common Life living in Weinbach, near Cologne, he said of the author: "He did not wish to name himself, and that will win him an eternal recompense; but Jesus knows his name well."

Since the seventeenth century 3 of the 25 supposed authors have remained contenders and, in general, we can say that the French have favored Jean Gerson, the Italians have promoted Giovanni Gersen, and the Dutch have acclaimed Thomas à Kempis. The dispute continues today but with less intensity than in former years, and most scholars are now inclined to recognize Thomas as the book's author.

The ascription of *The Imitation* to Jean Charlier de Gerson, renowned theologian and Chancellor of the University of Paris, seems natural since Gerson is known to have written several excellent treatises in ascetical theology. Such an attribution, however, appears untenable for these reasons: (a) *The Imitation* was clearly written by a monk for monks, and not by a university professor; (b) the theology advocated in *The Imitation* is that of the *Devotio moderna* or "New Devotion," as practiced in the Low Countries, and not the speculative scholastic theology taught at the University of Paris; and finally, (c) when Jean Gerson's younger brother made, under the chancellor's supervision, a catalog of his older brother's works, he made no mention of *The Imitation* as coming from his famous brother's pen.

The claim that Giovanni Gersen is the book's author is likewise untenable but for a more radical reason. Those who promote this claim assert that Gersen had been abbot of a monastery in Vercelli, Italy, but those who oppose it maintain (a) that these promoters have yet to offer definitive proof that Abbot Gersen existed and, furthermore, (b) Gersen's name does not appear on the known list of the abbots of Vercelli. That some Italian manuscripts bear the name Giovanni Gersen can be easily explained as an Italianization of Jean Gerson's name.

The evidence that favors Thomas a Kempis is more weighty. The best manuscript of the four books of *The Imitation* is bound together with nine other treatises certainly written by Thomas. This manuscript (no. 5855-61), preserved in the Royal Library of Brussels, is in Thomas' handwriting and bears at its end the notation: "Finished and completed in the year of our Lord, 1441. By the hand of Brother Thomas Kempis, at Mount St. Agnes, near Zwolle." This statement, it is true, does not explicitly state that Thomas is the author, nevertheless, the four books of *The Imitation* are joined to treatises definitely known to have been authored by Thomas.

In the book, *Illustrious Personages of Windesheim*, composed about 1464 and written by John Busch, a member of the same religious congregation as was Thomas, Busch notes that Thomas had once made a visit to Windesheim and describes him as "the author of several devotional treatises, especially 'He who follows me: on the imitation of Christ,' and other devout books." And when death interrupted Thomas' writing of *The Chronicles of the Canons Regular of Mount St. Agnes*, his successor in the task refers to him as "the author of diverse little books for the edification of the young, which were plain and simple in style, but mighty in content."

A close study of *The Imitation* itself reveals that (a) the author must have known Dutch, since he uses Dutch idioms; (b) he lived a communal life in a monastery; (c) he was imbued with the theology of the "New Devotion"; (d) he followed the custom of the Brethren of the Common Life by referring to his fellow monks as "the devout"; and, finally, (e) the style of *The Imitation* corresponds to that of Thomas' other known writings.

A new theory emerged in the Netherlands in 1924, stating that the true author of *The Imitation* was Master Gerard Groote (1340-1384), founder of the Brethren of the Common Life and of the "New Devotion." According to this theory, Gerard had written *The Imitation* as a personal spiritual diary and Thomas à Kempis had been asked to edit his writings, first in 1427, and then re-edited them in 1441. What argues against this theory is that (a) this ascription to Gerard was first made in the twentieth century and (b) there are no known contemporary manuscripts associating the work with him. Furthermore, (c) when Thomas came to write the founder's biography, he merely mentions that "Gerard wrote profitable treatises" and that he had translated two of John Ruysbroeck's works into Dutch. Since Gerard had been the esteemed founder of Thomas' congregation one would have expected Thomas to acknowledge him as the author of *The Imitation*, if he indeed were the author.

Thomas à Kempis

Thomas Hemerken was born in Kempen, near Düsseldorf, in the diocese of Cologne, Germany, toward the end of 1379 or in the first months of 1380. His early education was in the school operated by his mother, but in 1392, when he was 13 years old, he went to Deventer in the Low Countries to continue his studies; in this he was following in the steps of his older brother John, who had gone there some 12 years before. When the young Thomas arrived he learned that John was no longer in Deventer, but that he had joined the Brethren of the

Common Life, and since 1390 had been a canon at their monastery at Windesheim. So it was to Windesheim, some 20 miles north of Deventer, that Thomas went, and after meeting his brother and explaining his desire to study, John wrote a letter for Thomas to present to Master Florent Radewijns (+ 1400) in Deventer. Florent had been one of Gerard Groote's first disciples and had been won over to the "New Devotion" through Gerard's powerful preaching. This "New Devotion" did not mean that it was altogether novel or unheard of. Because the Catholics in the Low Countries had been slowly growing lax and tepid in the exercise of their faith, Gerard sought to renew in their hearts the faith that the Dutch formerly had, and thus Gerard's movement took on the name *Devotio moderna*, or "New Devotion." After Gerard's death in 1384, Florent succeeded him as the head of the Brethren in Deventer, and though he remained a canon in the local church, he continued to live in community with other clerics and several laymen all devoted to instilling the principles of the "New Devotion" in those among whom they worked.

When Thomas returned to Deventer he presented himself to Master Florent, who joyfully accepted him in his community until a suitable residence could be found for the young scholar in the city. At the same time, it was he who arranged for Thomas to attend the famous academy of John Boehm. Thomas' education in that Dutch city lasted 7 years, and when he had completed his studies in 1399, Florent suggested that he visit his brother John, who earlier that year had been elected prior of the recently founded monastery of Mount St. Agnes outside Zwolle.

Thomas visited his brother and, because he had grown familiar with the spirituality of the Brethren of the Common

Life through his constant association with Florent's community, requested admission into his brother's community. His wish was granted. From the outset Thomas, who was now known as Thomas of Kempen, or Thomas a Kempis in Latin, participated in the life of the canons, sharing their hours of prayer and work, and learning how to copy liturgical and devotional books, as well as manuscripts needed for their own library or for sale. It was in 1406, on the feast of Corpus Christi, that Thomas was formally accepted into the Congregation of the Canons Regular of St. Augustine and received its white habit, and then in 1408 he pronounced his religious vows. He was ordained to the priesthood in 1413, when he was 34 years old, and was elected sub-prior of the community in 1425. As sub-prior Thomas was not only the prior's assistant, but was also charged with the important task of instructing the young aspirants and novices in the way of the religious life. It is most probable that the four treatises that form *The Imitation* were written between 1420 and 1427, that is, during the years immediately preceding his appointment as sub-prior as well as the years in which he exercised that office.

Except for a three-year exile, Thomas spent his entire religious life at Mount St. Agnes. When Frederick of Blankenhem, Bishop of Utrecht, died in 1423, a dispute arose within the diocese as to who should be his successor. Several towns chose the nobleman Rudolph of Diepholt as bishop, but when Pope Martin V learned that Rudolph was not only illiterate but also an ignoramus, he confirmed Sweder of Culenborgh, dean of the cathedral chapter, as Frederick's successor. Since Sweder was unacceptable to the Rudolph faction, the dispute grew into open rebellion and in response to this disobedience Pope Martin placed the diocese under an interdict (1428). As a result of the interdict all public celebrations of Mass and the dispensing of sacraments were forbidden, except in the case of a dying person. Since the canons at Mount St. Agnes obeyed the papal interdict, and since the town of Zwolle was one of the few regions favoring Rudolph's appointment, open conflict arose between town and monastery, even to the point that the monks were threatened if they continued to withhold the sacraments. Preferring to remain obedient to the pope, the community voluntarily went into exile (June 1429) to Friesland, where it remained three years.

When the monks returned to Zwolle in 1432, Thomas was not among them. His brother John, who was then superior of the House of Bethany, near Arnheim, had become seriously ill, and in September 1431, Thomas left Friesland to care for him, remaining there until John's death on November 4, 1432, when he returned to his beloved Mount St. Agnes. During the ensuing years, Thomas served for a time as the community's procurator or treasurer, and then in 1448, when he was 69 years old, he was again elected sub-prior.

During Thomas' years in the community he made a copy of the entire Bible (1425-1439) in five volumes, still preserved in the Darmstadt Library. From his pen came some three dozen devotional works, among them: *The Soul's Soliloquy, On the Three Tabernacles, Prayers and Meditations on the Life of Christ, The Elevation of the Mind, The Garden of Roses,* and *On Solitude and Silence.* He likewise published the conferences he had given for novices under the title, *Sermons to Novices,* and wrote three biographies: of Master Gerard Groote, Master Florent Radewijns, and St. Lydwine. He was working on the history of Mount St. Agnes when he died. The monk who continued Thomas' chronicle wrote that Thomas died in 1471, on the feast of St. James the Less. This would have been on May 1; however, since St. James the Less shares his feast day with St. Philip, and the Windesheim liturgical calendar always calls it the feast of St. James and Philip, and never simply the feast of St. James the Less, scholars are of the opinion that the chronicler meant to write St. James the Greater, that is, *majoris*, but inadvertently wrote *minoris*. If this supposition is correct, then Thomas died on July 25, the date usually given for his death. He was 92 years old, and had been a religious for 65 years, and a priest for 58 years. He was buried in the monastery's east cloister. In 1560 the community gave up the monastery and in 1581 it was destroyed during the religious unrest in the Netherlands. Some 200 years after Thomas' burial, his remains were unearthed and in 1672 were reverently deposited in the church of St. Joseph in Zwolle. When that church fell into ruin, the remains were transferred in 1892 to the church of St. Michael, and are now revered in the new church of St. Michael, a short distance outside the old town of Zwolle.

The Imitation

The Imitation is made up of four distinct and independent treatises, written at different times, perhaps between 1420 and 1427. The work seems to have been composed for the spiritual benefit of the young religious at Mount St. Agnes. The early manuscripts of this masterpiece begin with the first two books in the order in which we find them published today, but the third and fourth are often interchanged. Since Thomas did not view these treatises as a single work, he did not give them a single title; the title that is most familiar to us, *The Imitation of*

Christ, derives from that of the first chapter of Book I. The book is also sometimes called *The Following of Christ*, and this comes from the words that begin that first chapter: "He who follows Me will not walk in darkness."

Thomas' four treatises were not intended as a theological exposition of the spiritual life; rather, he merely wanted to give his monks a series of meditative reflections on that life, pointing out how they could effectively pursue virtue, advance in the interior life, and attain union with Christ. He makes no appeal to our power of reasoning, but directs his words to our hearts and our desire to imitate Jesus Christ. In *The Imitation*, we neither seek intellectual stimulation nor new knowledge, but we look for strength and encouragement to continue in our resolve to be devout and holy.

Thomas clothes his thoughts in unusually simple language, and because he is sparse in his use of words, these thoughts have become, over the centuries, spiritual adages. Still, *The Imitation* was not meant to be a collection of such maxims, neither Thomas' own nor anyone else's. What Thomas offers us are the spiritual truths he has learned from the "New Devotion," gained from his praying over the Scriptures and from his reading of the Fathers of the Church and the lives of the saints, especially St. Augustine and St. Bernard. He gives us the fruit of his own experience, and tells us the way he himself learned to attain union with Christ. Though Thomas spent most of his life in the monastery, a reading of *The Imitation* makes clear his keen understanding of human nature and human psychology.

We would have liked it if Thomas had expanded many of his thoughts, nevertheless, this was Thomas' way of inviting us to reflect on what he has written. His simplicity is so profound that a single reading is insufficient for savoring all that he is trying to tell us. *The Imitation* cannot be read as other spiritual books are read, that is, several chapters in a single sitting. No, it must be read as the Bible is read, a chapter at a time with a period of meditation after each reading. The truths of this wonderful book must first make their entrance into our hearts, and then we must quietly reflect upon them so that they can truly become our own.

The reader will discover Thomas' love for and great familiarity with the Scriptures. Sometimes he quotes the holy text directly, but most often he paraphrases it, indicating that the text has become a part of his ordinary way of thinking. This present edition identifies Thomas' use of the Scriptures, but besides those that have been noted there are countless other words and phrases that the reader will immediately recognize as having their source in the Bible.

Book One of *The Imitation* is entitled "Helpful Counsels for the Spiritual Life" and has as its purpose the development of the interior man by renouncing all that is vain and illusory in the world, by disavowing all that delights the senses, and by advocating humility and the desire to be unknown. Thomas thus invites us to seek what is true, interior, and eternal. The book also contains several counsels particularly addressed to religious, but these have value for anyone seeking perfection in the spiritual life.

The title given to Book Two is "Directives for the Interior Life," and it continues and advances the theme of the First Book. We are told that the kingdom of God is found within us, and since that kingdom is internal it cannot be perceived by the external senses, nor can it be attained by any natural human affection, but only by a union with God through

Christ. "The true lover of Jesus and of truth is an inward man, and because he is free of all disordered affection he can freely turn to God and rise above himself in spirit and joyfully rest in Him" (chap. 2). Throughout this book, we are asked to give a ready ear to God's entreaties and Thomas instructs us that in order to be able to respond to God's call, we need humility, inner peace, purity of intention, vigilance over our natural inclinations, and a good conscience. He likewise wonderfully describes what it means to be a friend of Jesus, and ends the book with two powerful chapters, namely, "The Few Who Love the Cross of Jesus" (chap. 11), and "The Royal Road of the Holy Cross" (chap. 12).

Book Three is the longest of the books and carries the title "On Interior Consolation." It treats themes that have already been mentioned, but love and grace are now spoken of with greater frequency. Thomas has cast this book into the form of a dialogue between Jesus, the soul's Beloved, and the disciple, and the contents focus on the disciple's desire to ascend to God and to enjoy the divine delights. "When will that blessed and most desired of all hours come when You will fully satisfy me with Your presence, and be all in all to me? As long as this is not granted me, my joy will not be full" (chap. 34). The disciple seeks to be lost in God, and so enveloped in Christ's friendship that he can easily make a complete oblation of himself to his Creator and Lord. The rule operative throughout this book is: "My son, to the degree that you can leave yourself behind, to that degree will you be able to enter into Me. Just as desiring nothing outside you produces internal peace within you, so the internal renunciation of yourself unites you to God" (chap. 56).

The final book, "On the Blessed Sacrament," is much

different from the three preceding ones. It is presented as the peak of the doctrine contained in *The Imitation*. The Christian is now aware that the union he desires with God is sacramentally achieved on earth whenever he partakes of Christ's gift of His Body and Blood in the Eucharist. Like Book Three, this one is also in the form of a dialogue in which the disciple manifests his deep affection for Jesus and expresses his awareness that his growth in the spiritual life is furthered and enhanced by his reverence and love for the Blessed Sacrament.

The Translation

The best manuscript of Thomas à Kempis' *The Imitation of Christ* is, without doubt, his own autographed copy of 1441, preserved in Brussels. Thomas' manuscript remained at Mount St. Agnes until 1577, the year of the monastery's dissolution. At that time John Latome, superior of the Windesheim community, succeeded in saving the manuscript and presented it to a certain John Bellero, a friend of his who was a printer in Antwerp. Since Bellero had two sons who were members of the Society of Jesus, he gave the manuscript to the Antwerp Jesuits in 1590. With this masterpiece in their possession, the Jesuits decided to publish Thomas' writings and in 1600, under the editorship of H. Sommail, S.J., there appeared *Thomae a Kempis opera omnia ad autographa eiusdem*. It was this same Sommail who inserted the paragraph numbers that are in use today. The manuscript remained in the possession of the Antwerp Jesuits until 1773, the year of the Society's suppression, when it passed to the Royal Library in Brussels.

After Sommail's edition, other editions of Thomas' complete works followed, but the most recent has been that of Michael Joseph Pohl, *Thomae Hemerken a Kempis opera omnia* (Freiburg, 1902-1922), in 7 volumes. *The Imitation* is found in the second volume and it was Pohl's text of Thomas' 1441 autograph that served as the basis of the present translation. While using Pohl's text, I also made extensive use of J. B. M. Gence's *De imitatione Christi libri quatuor* published in Paris in 1821. Gence's text contains a wealth of information in its abundant notes.

While Thomas' Latin is direct and unembellished, he nevertheless succeeded in giving it a poetic quality. Besides rhymes that he sometimes used, Thomas delighted in parallel structures; I have reproduced these parallelisms in the present translation, and though unable to reproduce his rhymes, I have attempted to give the text a poetic cast. This translation claims fidelity to Thomas' thought, and while it intends to be modern it tries at the same time to retain its medieval and devotional flavor.

If the reader finds that this present translation has been an aid in his or her search for union with Jesus Christ, then the translator has received his reward. Finally, I would like to make my own the words that Thomas uses near the end of his masterpiece: "And after they shall have obtained the grace of devotion they desire and blissful union with You. . . may they prayerfully remember this spiritual pauper" (Book IV, chap. 17).

Solemnity of Mary and the
Giving of the Name Jesus

Joseph N. Tylenda, S.J.

BOOK I
Helpful Counsels for the Spiritual Life

1. *The Imitation of Christ and Contempt for the Vanities of the World*

He who follows Me will not walk in darkness,[1] says the Lord. These are the words of Christ by which He directs us to imitate His life and His ways, if we truly desire to be spiritually enlightened and free of all blindness of heart. Let it then be our main concern to meditate on the life of Jesus Christ.

2. Christ's teaching surpasses that of all the saints, and whoever has His spirit will find in His teaching *hidden manna.*[2] But it happens that many are little affected even after a frequent hearing of His Gospel; this is because they *do not have the spirit of Christ.*[3] If you want to fully understand Christ's words and to relish them, you must strive to conform your entire life to His.

3. What good does it do you to be able to give a learned discourse on the Trinity while you are without humility and, thus, are actually displeasing to the Trinity? Esoteric Words neither make us holy nor righteous; only a virtuous life makes us beloved of God. I would rather experience repentance in my soul than know how to define it.

If you memorized the whole Bible and knew all the maxims of the philosophers, what good would it do you if you were, at the same time, without God's love and grace? *Vanity of vanities! All is vanity,*[4] except our loving God and *serving only*

[1]John 8:12 [2]Rev. 2:17 [3]Rom. 8:9 [4]Eccles. 1:2

Him.[5] This is the highest wisdom: to despise the world and seek the kingdom of heaven.

4. It is vanity to seek riches that are sure to perish and to put your hope in them.

It is vanity to pursue honors and to set yourself up on a pedestal.

It is vanity *to follow the desires of the flesh*[6] and crave those things which will eventually bring you heavy punishment.

It is vanity to wish for a long life and to care little about leading a good life.

It is vanity to give thought only to this present life and not to the one that is to come.

It is vanity to love what is transitory and not to hasten to where everlasting joy abides.

5. Keep this proverb often in mind: *The eye is not satisfied with seeing, nor the ear filled with hearing.*[7] Therefore, withdraw your heart from the love of things visible and turn yourself to things invisible. Those who yield to their sensual nature dishonor their conscience and lose God's grace.

2. *Having a Humble Opinion of One's Self*

Everyone has a natural desire for knowledge[1] but what good is knowledge without the fear of God? Surely a humble peasant who serves God is better than the proud astronomer who knows how to chart the heavens' stars[2] but lacks all knowledge of himself.

[5]Deut. 6:13 [6]Gal. 5:16 [7]Eccles. 1:8

[1]Aristotle, *Metaphysics* I, 1 [2]Cf. Augustine, *Confessions* V, 4

If I truly knew myself I would consider myself insignificant and would not enjoy hearing others praise me. If I knew everything in the world and *were still without charity*,[3] what advantage would I have in the eyes of God who is to judge me according to my deeds?

2. Curb all undue desire for knowledge for in it you will find many distractions and much delusion. Those who are learned strive to give the appearance of being wise and desire to be recognized as such; but there is much knowledge that is of little or no benefit to the soul.

Whoever sets his mind on anything other than what serves his salvation is a senseless fool. A barrage of words does not make the soul happy, but a good life gladdens the mind and a *pure conscience*[4] generates confidence in God.

3. The more things you know and the better you know them, the stricter will God's judgment be, unless you have also lived a holier life. Do not boast about the learning and skills that are yours; rather, be somewhat circumspect since you do possess such knowledge.

4. If it seems to you that you know many things and thoroughly understand them all, realize that there are countless other things of which you are ignorant. *Be not haughty*,[5] but admit your ignorance. Why should you prefer yourself to another, when there are many who are more learned and better trained in God's law than you are? If you are looking for a knowledge and a learning that is useful to you, then love to be unknown[6] and be esteemed as nothing.

[3]1 Cor. 13:2 [4]1 Tim. 3:9 [5]Rom. 11:20

[6]In his *Third Sermon on Christmas Day* St. Bernard instructs his monks: "Love to be unknown."

5. This is the most important and most salutary lesson: to know and to despise ourselves. It is great wisdom and perfection to consider ourselves as nothing and always to judge well and highly of others. If you should see someone commit a sin or do some grievous wrong, do not think of yourself as someone better, for you know not how long you will remain in your good state.

We are all frail; but think of yourself as one who is more frail than others.

3. *The Teaching of Truth*

Happy is the individual whom Truth instructs, *not by means of obscure figures*[1] and fleeting words, but as it truly is in itself.

Our way of thinking and perceiving often misleads us and teaches us very little. What good is there in arguing about obscure and recondite matters when ignorance of such things will not be in question on the Day of Judgment? It is utter absurdity for us to neglect the things that are useful and necessary, and needlessly occupy ourselves with those that are only curious and perhaps harmful. *We have eyes but we do not see.*[2]

2. Why, indeed, should we concern ourselves with such philosophical words as *genera* and *species*? He whom the eternal Word teaches is set free from a multitude of frivolous theories. *From this one Word all things come into being;*[3] all things speak this one Word, and *this Word, who is the beginning, also speaks to us.*[4] Without this Word no one can understand or

[1]Num. 12:8 [2]Jer. 5:21 [3]John 1:3 [4]John 8:25

judge correctly. He to whom all things are one, and who refers all things to One, and sees all things in One, can remain steadfast in heart and abide in God's peace.

O God, my *Truth*,[5] make me one with You in *eternal love*.[6] I often become weary with reading and hearing many things; You are all that I want and desire. Let all teachers be mute and all creation keep silence before You; You, and only You, speak to me.

3. The more we are united to You and become inwardly simple, the more we can, and effortlessly too, understand sublime things about You, for we receive light and understanding from above.

He who has a pure, simple, and constant spirit is not distracted by the many things that he must do, but he does all for the honor of God and endeavors to remain inwardly free of all seeking of himself. What greater hindrance or annoyance is there than our heart's uncontrolled passions?

The good and devout person first inwardly plans the works that he will outwardly do. These works are not the result of any yielding to the desires of inferior nature but, on the contrary, he accomplishes them in accordance with the dictates of right reason.

No one undergoes a stronger struggle than the man who tries to subdue himself. This should be our chief employment: to strive to overcome ourselves and gain such a mastery that we daily grow stronger and better.

4. All perfection in this life has some imperfection mixed with it, and all intellectual reflection involves a certain amount of obscurity. A humble knowledge of yourself is a surer way to God than any deep scientific inquiry.

[5]John 14:6 [6]Jer. 31:3

Neither learning in general nor knowledge of even simple things ought to be condemned since they are something good in themselves and ordained by God; but a good conscience and a virtuous life are always to be preferred. Because many people spend more time and effort in becoming educated than in living properly, it happens that many, therefore, go astray and bear little or no fruit.

5. If we were as diligent in uprooting vices and planting virtues as we are in debating abstruse questions, there would not be so many evils or scandals among us nor such laxity in monastic communities. Certainly, when Judgment Day comes we shall not be asked what books we have read, but what deeds we have done; we shall not be asked how well we have debated, but how devoutly we have lived.

Tell me, where now are all those professors and doctors with whom you were once so well acquainted, when they were alive, and who were famous for their learning? Others hold their positions today and I doubt that these ever think of their predecessors. While they were alive they appeared to be men of influence, but today no one even mentions their names.

6. O, how quickly *the glory of the world evanesces!*[7] Would that their living had been equal to their learning; then they would have studied and lectured to good purpose.

How many perish in the world because of useless learning and for caring little about the service of God! Because they prefer to be famous rather than humble, *they lose themselves in intellectual acrobatics*[8] and come to nothing.

He is truly great who has abundant charity. He is truly great who is unimportant in his own eyes and considers the

[7] 1 John 2:17 [8] Rom. 1:21

greatest of honors a mere nothing. He is truly wise who esteems all earthly things as dung so that *he may gain Christ.*[9] Finally, he is truly the most learned who does God's will and abandons his own.

4. *Prudence in Our Actions*

We ought not to be too ready to believe every word[1] or item of gossip, but we ought to weigh each carefully and unhurriedly before God. Alas! Our weakness is such that we are often more inclined to believe and speak ill of someone than that which is good. But those who are perfect do not easily give credence to every tale they hear, for they know that human nature is prone to evil and that the *human tongue can be treacherous.*[2]

2. It is a mark of great wisdom neither to be hasty in our actions nor stubbornly maintain our private opinions. It is also wisdom neither to believe everything we hear, nor to pour it immediately into another's ear.

Seek counsel from one who is wise and honest[3] and ask instruction from one you esteem; do not follow your own devices. A good life makes us wise in the eyes of God and *makes us knowledgeable in many things.*[4] The humbler you are in heart and the more you submit yourself to God, the wiser will you be in everything, and greater peace will be yours.

[9]Phil. 3:8

[1]Sir. 19:15 [2]Sir. 14:1 [3]Tob. 4:18 [4]Sir. 34:9

5. *Reading the Holy Scriptures*

In Holy Scripture we seek truth and not eloquence. All Sacred Scripture should be read in the spirit with which it was written.

We should search the Scriptures for what is to our profit, rather than for niceties of language. You should read the simple and devout books as eagerly as those that are lofty and profound. The authority of the author, whether he be of great or little learning, ought not to influence you, but let the love of pure truth draw you to read them. Do not inquire about who is the one saying this, but pay attention to what he is saying.

2. Men enter and pass out of this world but the *faithfulness of the Lord endures forever.*[1] *God speaks to all of us in a variety of ways*[2] and is no respecter of persons. Our curiosity proves a hindrance to us for while reading the Scriptures we sometimes want to stop to debate and discuss, when we should simply read on.

If you wish to derive profit from your reading of Scripture, do it with humility, simplicity, and faith; at no time use it to gain a reputation for yourself as being one who is learned. Eagerly ask yourself questions and listen in silence to the words of the saints, and do not let the riddles of the ancients baffle you but, remember, they were written down for a definite purpose.

[1]Ps. 117:2 [2]Heb. 1:1

6. *Disordered Affections*

Whenever you desire anything inordinately, you immediately find that you grow dissatisfied with yourself. Those who are proud and avaricious never arrive at contentment; it is the poor and the humble in spirit who live their days in great peace.

Anyone who is not totally dead to himself will soon find that he is tempted and that he can be overcome by piddling and frivolous things. Whoever is weak in spirit, given to the flesh, and inclined to sensual things can, but only with great difficulty, drag himself away from his earthly desires. Therefore, he is often gloomy and sad when he is trying to pull himself from them and easily gives in to anger should someone attempt to oppose him.

2. If he has given in to his inclinations and has yielded to his passions, he is then immediately afflicted with a guilty conscience. In no way do such yieldings help him to find the peace he seeks. It is by resisting our passions, and not by being slaves to them, that true peace of heart is to be found.

There is no peace, therefore, in the heart of the man who is given to the flesh, nor in the man who is attached to worldly things. Peace is found only in one who is fervent and spiritual.

7. *Avoiding Vain Hope and Self-Conceit*

A fool is he who puts his trust in men[1] or created things. Do not be ashamed *to serve others for the love of Jesus Christ*[2] and to be reckoned as a poor man in this world.

[1]Jer. 17:5 [2]2 Cor. 4:5

Do not rely on yourself but place your trust in God. Do whatever lies in your power and God will assist your good intentions. Trust neither in your own knowledge nor in the craftiness of any human being; rather, trust in God's grace, *for it is He who supports the humble*[3] and humbles the overconfident.

2. *Glory neither in wealth,*[4] if you have any, nor in friends, if they are powerful, *but boast in God,*[5] the giver of all good things, who desires, above all, to bestow Himself on you.

Do not boast about your good looks nor your body's strength which a slight illness can mar and disfigure. Do not take pride in your skills and talents lest you offend God, to whom you owe these very gifts and endowments.

3. Do not esteem yourself as someone better than others lest, perhaps, you be accounted for worse in the eyes of God, *who knows what is in men's hearts.*[6] Take no pride in your good accomplishments for God judges differently than men and it often happens that what is displeasing to God is actually pleasing to men.

If you see anything good in yourself, believe still better things of others and you will, then, preserve humility. It will do you no harm if you account yourself as worst of all; but it will very much harm you to think that you are better than everyone else. The humble man dwells in unremitting peace while the heart of the proud man is filled with envy and resentment.

[3]James 4:6 [4]Jer. 9:23 [5]1 Cor. 1:31 [6]John 2:25

8. *Guarding Against Too Much Familiarity*

Do not reveal your thoughts to everyone,[1] but *discuss your affairs with one who is wise*[2] and fears God. Do not associate too freely with young people nor with strangers. Do not flatter those who are rich, nor be eager to be *in the presence of those who are important in the eyes of the world.*[3]

Keep company with the humble and simple, with the devout and godly, and speak of those things which nurture religion. Do not be familiar with any woman but, in general, commend all good women to God.[4] Desire to be familiar only with God and His angels and shun the acquaintance of men.

2. We must have charity toward all but familiarity is not necessary. It sometimes happens that a person unknown to us enjoys a dazzling reputation, but when we finally do meet he makes much less of an impression. We sometimes think that our own presence gives pleasure to others, whereas we may really be offensive to them because of some unbecoming behavior in us.

9. *Obedience and Submission*

It is a very excellent thing to be under obedience, that is, to live under a superior and not to be one's own master. There is greater security in living a life of submission than there is in exercising authority. Many live under obedience, more out of necessity than out of love of God, and they murmur and complain in their discontent. These will never achieve spiri-

[1]Sir. 8:19 [2]Sir. 9:15 [3]Prov. 25:6 [4]Cf. Sir. 9:1-13

tual freedom until, for the love of God, they submit themselves with all their heart.

No matter where you go, here or there, you will find no rest except in humbly subjecting yourself to the authority of a superior. Many have dreamed that it would be better for them to be in another monastery, but they found they were deluded.

2. It is indeed true that everyone likes to have his own way and is partial to those who think the same as he does. But if God dwells among us then we must sometimes relinquish our own opinion for the sake of peace. Who is so wise as to be able to know all things? Therefore, rely not too heavily on your own opinion, but listen to the ideas of others as well. Your opinion may be a good one but if, for God's sake, you set it aside and follow that of another, you will profit the more.

3. I have often heard it said that *it is safer to listen and to take advice*[1] than to offer it. It may well happen that each one's opinion is good, but to refuse to go along with another's opinion, when reason or a just cause demand it, is a sign of perverse pride.

10. Guarding Against Unnecessary Speech

Avoid the gatherings of men as much as you can. The discussion of worldly affairs, even though engaged in with good intentions, is nevertheless a hindrance, for we quickly become tainted and charmed by trivia. I have often wished that I had remained silent and had not been in the company of men.

[1]Prov. 12:15

Why are we so fond of speaking and conversing with one another, though we rarely return to our silence without some injury to our consciences? The reason why we enjoy talking is because we seek solace in chatting with one another, and desire to lighten our distracted hearts. Furthermore, we enjoy talking and thinking about those things we most want and desire, or those which we especially dislike.

2. But alas! It is often vain and to no purpose, for the consolation gained by talking greatly diminishes the internal consolation granted us by God. Therefore, *we must watch and pray*[1] lest we spend our time in fruitless idleness.

If it is permitted and advisable to speak, then speak *of those things that nourish the spiritual life.*[2] Negligence about our spiritual progress and yielding to bad habits are the reasons for our keeping so little control over our tongues. Godly conversation about spiritual matters very much helps spiritual advancement, especially when persons of like mind and heart are united in God.

11. Achieving Peace and Acquiring Zeal for One's Spiritual Progress

Much peace could be ours if we did not occupy ourselves with what others say and do, for such things are of no concern to us. How can we long remain in peace if we involve ourselves in other people's business, if we seek outside distractions, and if we are rarely, or only to a small degree, interiorly recollected? Blessed are they who keep to themselves, for they shall enjoy much peace.

[1]Matt. 26:41 [2]Eph. 4:29

2. How did some of the saints become so perfect and expert in contemplative prayer? They made it their duty to restrain their every earthly desire and, thus, they were free to cling to God with all their heart and to attend to their soul's welfare. We are much too taken up with our own passions and much too anxious about ephemeral things. We seldom succeed in overcoming as much as a single fault, and we are not wholly on fire with the desire to make daily spiritual progress. The result is that we remain negligent and tepid.

3. If we were altogether dead to ourselves, and our hearts were free of all entanglements, then we might be able to savor the things of God and contemplate heavenly realities. Our biggest and most difficult barrier to advancement is that we have not liberated ourselves from our passions and sensual desires, nor are we trying to walk in the blameless way of the saints. Whenever we encounter some small adversity we much too quickly yield to discouragement and look around us for human consolation.

4. If, like valiant men, we labored to stand firm in the fray, certainly we would experience the Lord's heavenly protecting help. He stands ready to aid those who fight and who place their trust in His grace — it is He who provides us with these conflicts and He wants us to be the victors. But if we base our spiritual progress only on performing external actions, then our devotion will soon come to an end. We must *put the axe to the root*[1] so that, purified from all passion, we may achieve peace of mind.

5. If we eradicated one vice a year we should soon become perfect men. But often we see the opposite happen: we find we were better and more fault-free at the time of our conversion

[1]Matt. 3:10

to God[2] than many years afterwards. Our eagerness and progress in virtue ought to increase each and every day, but today it is judged an accomplishment if a man retains something of his first fervor! If we had treated ourselves a bit more harshly in the beginning, we might afterwards have been able to accomplish everything with joyful ease.

6. It is difficult to give up old habits and still more difficult to go against one's own will. But if you do not overcome small and easy things, when will you overcome those that are larger and more troublesome? Resist your inclination at the very beginning and break off that habit; otherwise, little by little, it will lead you into greater problems.

If you only knew how much peace you can give yourself and how much joy to others by living as you should, I think you would show greater interest in your spiritual progress.

12. *The Uses of Adversity*

Sometimes it is to our advantage to endure misfortunes and adversities, for they make us enter into our inner selves and acknowledge that we are in a place of exile and that we ought not to rely on anything in this world. And sometimes it is good for us to suffer contradictions and know that there are those who think ill and badly of us, even though we do our best and act with every good intention. Such occasions are aids in keeping us humble and shield us from pride. When men ridicule and belittle us we should turn to God, who sees our

[2]In the Middle Ages "conversion to God" was synonymous with "entering a monastery." The *conversi* included monks as well as those who lived and worked in the monastery but were without monastic vows.

innermost thoughts, and seek His judgment.

2. Therefore, we should so firmly establish ourselves in God that we have no need to seek much human encouragement. It is when a man of good will is distressed, or tempted, or afflicted with evil thoughts, that he best understands the overwhelming need he has for God, *without whom he can do nothing.*[1] While enduring these afflictions he takes himself to prayer with sighs and groans; he grows tired of this life and wishes to die so that *he could be undone in order to live with Christ.*[2] It is in such times of trial that he realizes that perfect security and full peace are not to be found in this world.

13. *How To Resist Temptation*

As long as we live in this world it is impossible for us to be without trials and temptations. Thus, Job writes: *Is not man's life on earth a drudgery?*[1] Everyone, therefore, should show great concern about his temptations and *watch and pray lest the devil, who never sleeps but prowls about, finds an opportunity to ensnare him.*[2] No one is so perfect or so holy as to be without some temptation; nor can we ever be totally free of them.

2. Though temptations may be troublesome and a burden, nevertheless, they often prove very profitable, for through them we are humbled, purified, and disciplined. The saints have all experienced trials and temptations and have gained by them; those who were unable to bear them have fallen away and have become lost. There is no religious order so holy, nor place so isolated, where trials and temptations are unknown.

3. We are never entirely free of temptations — no matter

[1]John 15:5 [2]Phil. 1:23 [1]Job 7:1 [2]1 Pet. 5:8

how long we live — because we carry their very source within us. We have all been born with concupiscence.[3] When one temptation or trial passes, another comes, and we shall always have something to suffer because we have all lost our original happiness.

Many attempt to flee temptations but they only sink more deeply into them. Conflicts are not won by running away; rather, it is by humbly and patiently standing up to them that we gain strength against all our enemies.

4. He who only superficially trims his temptations and does not pull them out by their roots advances little. The temptations will only return the sooner and he will find himself in a more deplorable condition. *With patient endurance*[4] and with God's help, little by little, you will better conquer them, than by frantically reacting to them. When temptations do come, seek counsel frequently, and when someone else is tempted do not treat him harshly but, on the contrary, console and encourage him. Show him the same kindness you yourself would like to receive.

5. The beginning of all evil temptation lies in a flighty mind and insufficient trust in God. Just as a rudderless ship is buffeted back and forth by the waves, so the negligent and inconstant man is smitten by many temptations. *As fire tests iron,*[5] so temptation tests the righteous man. Often we are unaware of what we can actually accomplish; it is through temptation that we discover what we really are.

We must be especially on our guard at the beginning of temptation, for then we can more easily overcome the enemy if we refuse him entrance into our mind and, keeping him outside on the doorstep, confront him at his first knock.

[3]Cf. James 1:14 [4]Col. 1:11 [5]Sir. 31:26

Someone once said: "Resist at the very outset; it is much too late to apply remedies after the patient has become critically ill."[6] Temptation, at first, is but a simple thought in the mind; the imagination then embellishes it and it takes on the appearance of something quite desirable; then follows a powerful attraction and finally the will's consent. The depraved enemy gradually gains entrance if he is not resisted at the very beginning. The more sluggish our resistance, the more vulnerable we daily become, and the more powerful does our adversary grow.

6. Some individuals suffer greater temptations at the time of their conversion to God, while others suffer them toward the end of their life, and there are those who are afflicted throughout their entire lifetime. Some are but only slightly tempted and this is according to God's wise and just designs, who always takes into account our human condition and worthiness, and orders all things unto the salvation of His elect.

7. Therefore, we must not yield to despair during temptation, but pray the more earnestly to God, asking Him to support us in our every trial, remembering the words of St. Paul: *with the temptation God will also provide the way of escape, that you may be able to endure it.*[7] In all trials and temptations *let us then meekly place ourselves before God*[8] who has promised to save and *raise on high those who humble themselves in spirit.*[9]

8. A man's spiritual progress is put to the test by trials and temptations, and by resolutely bearing up under them he not only gains greater merit but gives evidence of his virtue. There is nothing remarkable in a devout and fervent man being without trials, but if he suffers patiently in time of adversity,

[6]Ovid, *Remedies for Love,* v. 91 [7]1 Cor. 10:13
[8]Judith 8:17 [9]Luke 1:52

then, there is hope for great spiritual advancement.

Some individuals are preserved from great temptations but often are vanquished by those unimportant ones we meet every day. This is surely intended to humble them, that they may know that, being weak in trifling matters, they ought never rely only upon themselves in more serious ones.

14. Avoiding Hasty Judgments

Keep your eyes on yourself and avoid judging the actions of others. In judging others we accomplish nothing, are often in error, and readily fall into sin; but we always gain by self-examination and self-criticism.

Our judgments frequently depend on our likes and dislikes and thus are far from true because we make them conform to our personal prejudices. If God were our one and only desire we would not be so easily upset when our opinions do not find outside acceptance.

2. It often happens that there is some hidden motive within us, or some outside influence acting upon us, that leads us to make such judgments. Countless are the individuals who seek themselves in all they put their hand to, but are quite unaware of the fact. They appear to be satisfied and tranquil as long as everything goes according to their wishes and desires, but as soon as something goes wrong they quickly become disturbed and depressed. Such divergence in ideas and opinions is frequently the cause of quarrels among friends and acquaintances, and likewise among religious and the devout.[1]

[1]The spirituality prevalent in the Netherlands in the late fourteenth and fifteenth centuries was the *Devotio moderna*, whose chief exponent was Gerard

3. Old habits are relinquished only with difficulty and no one wants to be led any further than he can see in front of him. If you rely more on your own reasoning and logic than on the conquering power of Jesus Christ, then you will tardily, if ever, become spiritually enlightened. God desires our complete subjection to Him and wants our passionate love of Him to transcend our reasoning.

15. *Works Done with Charity*

An evil deed ought never be done for anything in the world nor for the love of any human being. For the benefit of someone in need, however, a good work may, at times, be set aside and a better one substituted in its place; thus, a good work is not avoided but transformed into something more excellent.

An external deed done without charity is without value, but when performed with charity — no matter how small or insignificant the action be — it becomes meritorious. God notes the love that impels the action and not the number of works done. He does much who loves much.

2. He does much who does well what he does, and who serves the common good rather than his own will. What sometimes passes for charity is really yielding to one's natural inclinations, and among the motives are self-interest, personal preference, and hope of reward.

Groote (1340-1384), founder of the Brethren of the Common Life. Those who followed this spirituality called themselves "the devout." Thomas may be referring to quarrels that may have arisen between the members of his community and other religious houses.

3. Whoever possesses true and perfect charity does not seek himself in anything, but desires God's glory in all things. The truly charitable man envies no one since he seeks no personal joy, nor does he find happiness in himself but wishes to be made happy only in God. To no man does he attribute goodness but only to God, from whom all things proceed as from their source, and in whom the saints find their joy and final rest.

If we had a spark of true charity within us we would surely perceive the emptiness of all earthly things.

16. *Bearing with One Another's Failings*

Whatever we are unable to reform in ourselves or in others, we must clearly put up with until God chooses to change it. View this as being, perhaps, the better state, for by undergoing this test it teaches us patience without which all our actions carry little merit. And while enduring these misfortunes, pray God to grant you His support that you may quietly bear them.

2. If anyone, after having been corrected once or twice, still does not conform, do not take issue with him, but commit the matter to God so that God's will may be done and that He may be honored in all His servants. After all, God alone knows how to draw good out of evil.[1]

Be patient in bearing the imperfections and weaknesses of others, no matter what they be, just as others have to put up with your faults. If you cannot remake yourself in the way you would like why, then, do you expect another to fashion himself according to the pattern you set for him? We want

[1]Cf. Gen. 50:20

others to be perfect, but we do nothing to amend our own faults.

3. We want others to be properly corrected, but take umbrage when someone corrects us. We are annoyed at another's freedom as being too ample, but want nothing denied us. We would have others bound by laws, but want no curbs set on our lives. It is frightfully evident, then, that we use one scale to weigh our neighbors and another for ourselves. If we were all perfect then there would be nothing for us to suffer from the hands of others for the love of God!

4. But God has willed that we learn to *bear one another's burdens.*[2] *Each of us has some failing and some trial to bear*[3] and *none of us has the strength to bear them by himself,*[4] *nor the wisdom.*[5] Therefore, we must *bear with one another,*[6] *comfort each other,*[7] support, instruct, and advise one another.

The quality of a man's virtue is best displayed in difficult times, and far from weakening him, such times reveal him for what he really is.

17. The Monastic Life

If you wish to keep peace and live in harmony with others, you must learn to abdicate your will in many things. It is no small matter to live in a monastery or a congregation and abide there without complaint and *persevere faithfully until death.*[1] Blessed is he who has well lived the monastic life and has brought it to a happy end.

If you want to persevere and make spiritual progress look

[2]Gal. 6:2 [3]Gal. 6:5 [4]2 Cor. 3:5 [5]Prov. 3:7
[6]Col. 3:13 [7]1 Thes. 5:11 [1]Rev. 2:10

upon yourself as *an exile and a pilgrim on this earth*[2] and, in addition, if you wish to lead the religious life you must be willing to become *a fool for the sake of Christ.*[3]

2. To wear a monk's habit and to have one's head tonsured produces little change in the monk himself. What truly distinguishes the real religious are his change in outlook on life and the complete control of his passions.

He who seeks anything in the monastery other than God and his soul's salvation will find nothing but sadness and misery, and he who strives not to be the least of all and the servant to all,[4] will not enjoy peace very long.

3. You have entered the monastery to obey and not to govern,[5] and know that you are called to suffer and labor and not spend your time in idle and empty gossip. Here, in the monastery, men are tried *as gold is tried in the furnace,*[6] and no one can remain here unless he is willing, with his whole heart, to humble himself for the love of God.

18. *The Examples of the Holy Fathers*

Study the worthy examples of the holy Fathers, those illustrious models of true perfection and devotion, and you will conclude that you are doing very little or almost nothing. What is our life when compared to theirs! These saints and friends of Christ served the Lord in hunger and thirst, in cold and nakedness, in labor and fatigue, in night vigils and fasts, in

[2]Heb. 11:13 [3]1 Cor. 4:10 [4]Cf. Luke 22:26

[5]St. Bernard, writing to Pope Eugene III, reminds him that "a ministry has been imposed upon [him] rather than a dominion bestowed." *On Consideration* II, 9. [6]Wis. 3:6

prayers and holy meditation, in persecutions and countless insults.

2. How numerous and how severe were the trials undergone by the apostles, martyrs, confessors, virgins, and others who chose to follow in Christ's footsteps! How little they thought of their lives in this world *that they might possess them for all eternity*![1]

How strict and full of renunciation was the life these holy Fathers lived in the desert! What long and arduous temptations they had to suffer! How often the adversary harassed them! How frequently and earnestly they prayed to God! How scrupulously they kept their fasts!

What eagerness and application they manifested in their desire for spiritual progress! How valiant the contest they fought to eradicate their faults! How pure and righteous their determination to love God! They spent their days in labor and their nights in long prayers — even their working hours were not without mental prayer.

3. They spent their time gainfully. Every hour spent with God seemed all too brief, and in experiencing the great sweetness of contemplating God they forgot their body's need for nourishment. They renounced all wealth, dignities, honors, friends, and family; they desired absolutely nothing of this world. They barely accepted what was necessary to sustain life and only begrudgingly did they partake of it.

In earthly things they were poor, but in grace and virtue they were opulent. Outwardly they were in want, but inwardly they regaled in God's consoling grace.

4. They were strangers to this world but close and intimate friends of God. They saw themselves as nothing and the world

[1]John 12:25

despised them, but in the sight of God they were priceless and beloved. They possessed true humility, lived in simple obedience, and walked in charity and patience, and thus they daily progressed in spirit and found great favor with God. These holy Fathers are given as models to us religious and their examples more powerfully spur us on to advance in holiness than the multitude of the lukewarm can entice us to become lax.

5. O how great was the fervor of all religious at the founding of their holy institute! How great was their devotion in prayer and zeal for virtue! How faithful they were in observing the rule! How admirably reverence and obedience flourished under a superior! The reputations they left behind them bear witness that they were men of true greatness and holiness, who battled heroically and successfully trampled the world under their feet. Nowadays we extol to the heavens the one who merely keeps the rule and suffers, with resignation, the life he himself has chosen to live!

6. O how lukewarm and indifferent we find ourselves in our present condition! How quickly we slip from our first fervor and through slothfulness and carelessness grow tired of our way of life! I hope the desire for advancement in virtue is not asleep in you, who have so often seen these many worthy examples of devoted men.

19. The Exercises of a Good Religious

The life of a good religious must abound with every virtue so that he can inwardly be what he outwardly professes to be. In fact, he ought to possess greater interior virtue than he externally manifests because God's eyes are always upon us, and it is He whom we must reverence in all places and, like the angels, we must walk in innocence before Him.

Each day we ought to renew our resolves and rekindle the fires of our fervor as if it were the first day of our conversion. And we should say: "O Lord God, help me to keep my good resolution to serve You; give me the grace to begin anew for what I have done up to now is nothing."

2. Our spiritual advancement will equal our resolutions, so if we want to make good spiritual progress we need to exercise diligence in making our resolves. If the man who makes his resolutions with stout-heartedness often fails, then what about the one who makes them only feebly and infrequently?

Failure to keep resolutions results from a variety of reasons, and every seemingly unimportant omission in our spiritual practices produces some injury. The resolutions of a righteous man depend on God's grace and not on his own wisdom, and whatever he undertakes to do he must first place his trust in Him. *Man proposes, but God disposes!*[1] Furthermore, the *course of a man's life is not left to the man himself.*[2]

3. If a prescribed exercise is omitted because of a brother in need, or because we must perform some other charitable deed, the exercise may be fulfilled at a later time; but if we omit it without good reason or out of laziness, then it is no small fault and it will prove harmful to us. Though we try our best we find that we still fail in many things; hence, we must make our resolutions specific and especially with regard to those things that are our greatest obstacles to progress. We must examine both our inner thoughts and our external actions and put

[1]Prov. 16:9 [2]Jer. 10:23

them in order, for both have an important part to play in our spiritual advancement.

4. If you cannot be continually recollected then at least be so at certain times, for example, in the morning and in the evening. In the morning make your resolution, and in the evening examine your performance, checking how you conducted yourself during the day. Scrutinize your speech, your actions, and your thoughts, because by these means you may have offended God and your neighbor.

Arm yourself like the man who prepares himself to resist the devil's temptations;[3] keep your love for food in check and you will find it easier to control all inclinations of the flesh. Never be altogether idle but read or write, pray or meditate, or do something worthwhile for the community.

5. Use discretion in undertaking bodily penances and everyone should not practice the same ones. Penances that do not pertain to community life should not be done in public, and those that are of your own choosing should be performed in private.

See to it that you are not negligent in performing community exercises and overhasty in performing those of your own choice, but after you have faithfully fulfilled those to which you are bound by rule, or have been commanded to perform, then, and if time allows, give yourself to those that your own devotion suggests.

The one and the same practice is not for everyone; it may suit one individual but not another. Also, a variety of practices fit a variety of times; some are more suitable for feast days while others are more appropriate for weekdays. One is good

[3]Eph. 6:11

in time of temptation, another in time of peace and calm; one when we are depressed, another when we are happy in the Lord.

6. On the great feast days our religious practices should refresh our spirits and make us more earnestly implore the intercession of the saints. We should live from one feast to another, and make our resolutions as if on the following feast we were to leave this world for the eternal feast. Therefore, during these festival seasons we ought to prepare ourselves to live more devoutly, and to observe our rules more faithfully, as if we were soon to receive from God the reward of our labor.

7. If that reward be deferred, then know that we are not sufficiently prepared and are still unworthy of that great *glory which is to be revealed to us*[4] at the appointed time, and let us use what time we have to make better preparation for our departure. The evangelist Luke writes: *Blessed is that servant whom the master finds awake when he comes; truly, I tell you, he will set him over all his possessions.*[5]

20. *The Love of Silence and Solitude*

Set aside an opportune time for deep personal reflection and think often about God's many benefits to you. Give up all light and frivolous matters, and read what inspires you to repentance of soul and not what just entertains the mind.

If you abstain from unnecessary conversation and useless visiting, as well as from listening to idle news and gossip, you will find sufficient and suitable times for your meditations. The great saints avoided the company of men as much as they

[4]Rom. 8:18 [5]Luke 12:37, 42

could, because they wanted to live for God in silence.

2. Someone once said: "As often as I have been out among men, I have returned less a man."[1] We experience the very same thing when we talk overlong. It is easier to be completely silent than to refrain from talking too much; it is easier to remain at home than to be always on one's guard when in public.

If you aim at a fervent spiritual life then you too must turn your back on the crowds as Jesus did.[2] The only man who can safely appear in public is the one who wishes he were at home. He alone can safely speak who prefers to be silent. Only he can safely govern who prefers to live in submission, and only he can safely command who prefers to obey.

3. No one can be unfailingly happy unless he has *the assurance of a good conscience.*[3] The saints enjoyed this security but fear of God had a good part in it, and just because they possessed great virtue and received special graces, it did not mean that they could be any less diligent or humble. The wicked also feel secure, but their security is born of pride and presumption, and ends in self-deception. Though you may appear to be a model religious, or even a holy hermit, never look upon yourself as totally secure as long as you are in this world.

4. Those who are highly esteemed by others risk great danger by becoming overconfident. Therefore, it is better for us not to be wholly free of temptation, but to be frequently assailed and, thus, we will not seek assurance in ourselves, nor become bloated with pride, nor too readily seek consolation from the world.

[1]Seneca, *Epistle* 7 [2]Cf. Mark 6:31; Luke 5:16

[3]2 Cor. 1:12

How undisturbed a conscience we would have if we never went searching after ephemeral joys nor concerned ourselves with the affairs of the world! What great peace and tranquility would be ours if we had severed ourselves from useless preoccupations, put our trust in God, and thought only of divine things and our salvation!

5. The man who has not diligently practiced holy repentance is not worthy of heavenly consolations. If you want to experience this repentance in your heart, go to your room and shut out the din of the world, as it is written: *commune with your own hearts on your beds and be silent.*[4] Retire to your room and there you will preserve what you usually lose by leaving it.

If you keep to your room you will find delight in it, but if you only visit it, it becomes irksome and annoying. If, at the time of your conversion, you had accustomed yourself to stay in your room and remain there, it would now be your good friend and a source of great pleasure to you.

6. The devout man makes progress in the silent and quiet reading of the Scriptures wherein he learns many hidden things. In them he discovers an abundance of tears which daily purify him, and the farther away he is from the world's tumult, the more familiar he becomes with his Creator. Whoever withdraws himself from dealing with men, that man God draws to Himself and to His holy angels.

It is better to lead a hidden life and care about one's salvation than to neglect it and work miracles. The religious who rarely goes out, avoids being seen, and is unwilling to see others, is the one who is worthy of praise.

[4]Ps. 4:4

7. Why do you desire to see what is not lawful for you to have? *The world and all its allurements pass away.*[5] Sensual desire entices you to ramble about, and when your roaming is over what do you bring back with you but a dissipated conscience and a distracted heart?

A joyous departure often results in a sad return, and a jovial evening makes a somber morning. So it is with all the pleasures of the flesh. Their entrance is quite enjoyable, but *in the end they sting and kill.*[6] What can you see in some other place that you do not see right here? Here you have the heavens, the earth, and all the elements; after all, from these same things everything else is made.

8. Can you find anything anywhere *that can long remain under the sun*?[7] You think you will find contentment, but you will never achieve it. If, with a single glance, *you could see everything in the world spread out before your eyes, how fruitless a sight that would be!*[8] Raise your eyes to God on high and pray for your sins and deficiencies. Leave hollow things for hollow people, but you fulfill those things that God has commanded you.

Shut the door of your room[9] and call Jesus, your Beloved, to you, and stay there with Him. There is no greater peace anywhere else than to be with Jesus. If you had not left your room, nor listened to gossip, you would have retained your peace, but because you crave the latest news you must, as a consequence, suffer a disordered heart.

[5]1 John 2:17 [6]Prov. 23:32 [7]Eccles. 2:11 [8]Eccles. 1:14
[9]Matt. 6:6

21. Repentance of Heart

If you wish to make spiritual progress *live in the fear of the Lord.*[1] Do not be easygoing, but control and govern your senses and do not give yourself over to foolish merrymaking. Apply yourself to repentance of heart and you will find devotion. Repentance opens the way to much good while dissipation quickly destroys it. It is unthinkable that a man can truly find happiness in this life if at the same time he views himself as an exile here and sees his soul surrounded by many dangers.

2. Because our hearts are frivolous and because we ignore our faults we never discover the sickness in our souls, but idly we laugh when we have full reason to weep. The only true liberty or honest joy is in fearing God with a good conscience.

Blessed is the man who can set aside all sources of distraction and perfectly recollect himself in holy repentance. Blessed is he who shuns all that soils and weighs down his conscience. Act with courage, for habit is broken by habit. If you leave men alone they, in turn, will leave you alone to do what you have to do.

3. Do not interfere in other men's business, nor meddle in the affairs of those who are more important than you. Always keep an eye on yourself and be more willing to correct yourself than your dearest friends.

Do not be upset if you do not enjoy men's favor, rather, your main interest should be that you behave thoughtfully and prudently as becomes a servant of God and a good religious.

It is often better and safer for us not to give too many

[1]Prov. 19:23

comforts to our bodies in this life. However, if we are without the comforts of God, or rarely have them, then it is our own fault because we neither desire repentance of heart nor do we wholly despise the shallow comforts of this world.

4. Remember that you are undeserving of heavenly consolations and deserving of many trials. When your repentance becomes perfect, the whole world becomes tiresome and repulsive.

A good man always finds sufficient matter for his sorrow and his tears. Whether he thinks of himself or of his neighbor, he knows that no one dwells on this earth without some trials. And the more thoroughly he reflects upon himself, the more intense does his sorrow grow. Our sins should be the object of true sorrow and interior repentance, as well as our failings which have so tightly entangled us that we are seldom able to contemplate divine things.

5. If you gave more frequent thought to your death than to a long life, you would unquestionably be more eager to amend your life. If you gave serious reflection to future punishments, either of hell or purgatory, I think you would more willingly put up with toil and sadness, nor would you recoil from any hardship. Because these thoughts never penetrate our hearts, and because we still love all that pleases our senses, we lazily remain in our apathy.

6. Indeed, it is because our hearts lack courage that this miserable body of ours complains so easily. Therefore, humbly pray to the Lord for the spirit of repentance, and say with the Prophet: *Feed me with the bread of tears and give me tears to drink in full measure.*[2]

[2]Ps. 80:5

22. *Reflection on Human Wretchedness*

Wherever you are, and wheresoever you turn, you are wretched unless you turn to God.

Why be disturbed if things do not succeed according to your plans and desires? Who is there that gets everything according to his likes? Neither I, nor you, nor anyone else on this earth. No man in this world is without some trial or affliction, not even a king or a pope. Who, then, has it the best? He who is willing to suffer for God's sake.

2. Half-witted and feeble-minded people often remark: "Look what a happy life that man has! See how rich, how great, how powerful and influential he is!" But if you have eyes for heavenly things you will perceive that all temporal goods are mere trifles. They are unpredictable and highly troublesome because you can never possess them without some anxiety and apprehension. Our happiness does not consist in having temporal goods in abundance; a moderate amount will suffice our needs.

It is indeed wretched to live upon this earth. The more a man desires to be spiritual, the more distaste he has for the present life since he better understands and more keenly detects the foibles and faults of human nature. Man must eat and drink, sleep and be alert, labor and rest, and be subject to all the other demands of nature, and all these are a great misery and source of sadness for the devout man who longs to be released and set free from sin.

3. The spiritual man is greatly loaded down by his bodily needs. Thus the Prophet sincerely prays to be free of them, saying: *Bring me out of my distresses.*[1] But woe to those who are

[1]Ps. 25:17

not aware of their wretchedness, and more so to those who love this pitiable and wretched life. There are some who love it so passionately that even if their daily labor or begging barely provided them with life's necessities, they would still want to live here rather than think of the kingdom of God.

4. O unreasonable and unbelieving men, to have ensconced yourselves so deeply in earthly goods as to relish nothing but the things of the flesh! Wretched fools! You will discover to your sorrow that the object of your love is something vile and worthless.

But the saints of God and all the faithful friends of Christ scorn what pleases the flesh and what thrives and flourishes in this world, and have directed all their hope toward eternal things. All their desires tended heavenwards, to things invisible and everlasting, lest the love of things visible should drag them down and bind them here below.

Do not despair, brother, of making spiritual progress; there is still time and the hour has not yet passed.

5. Why do you postpone making your resolutions day after day? Come now, and begin this very moment and say to yourself: "*Now is the time to do it;*[2] now is the time to fight; now is the right time to amend my life." When you are afflicted and troubled, that is the time for merit. You must pass through fire and water before you arrive at redemption. Unless you do violence to yourself, you will not overcome your faults.

As long as we have this frail body with us we cannot be without sin, nor live without anxiety and grief. We would indeed like to be free of all wretchedness, but because we have lost our innocence through sin, we have at the same time lost true happiness. Therefore, *we must exercise patience*[3] and await

[2] 2 Cor. 6:2 [3] Heb. 10:36

God's mercy until the storms have passed, and *until our mortal bodies are swallowed up by life.*[4]

6. How great is our human frailty and how prone to evil! You confess your sins today, and tomorrow you commit the very same ones. Right now you resolve to be on your guard, and an hour from now you will act as though you never made any resolution whatever. Since we are so frail and vacillating, we have good reason to humble ourselves and never to think highly of ourselves. And it can happen that through our negligence we lose what we have gained after much labor and time and through God's grace.

7. What will become of us later on if we become lukewarm so early? Woe to us if we are yielding to rest, as if we had already *achieved peace and safety*[5] when, in reality, our behavior manifests no signs of true holiness. We ought to become novices once more and again be instructed in the principles of good religious behavior and then, perhaps, there might be some hope for future amendment and greater spiritual progress.

23. *Meditation on Death*

A short time is all that you have here. What is in store for you afterwards? Here today, gone tomorrow![1] When out of sight, you are soon out of mind.

How dull and insensible is man's heart thinking only of the present and not caring about what is to come! Your every thought and action should be that of a man who is to die this day. If you had a good conscience you would not especially

[4]2 Cor. 5:4 [5]1 Thes. 5:3

[1]Cf. 1 Macc. 2:63

fear death; indeed, it is easier to fly from sin than to flee death.

If you are not prepared to die today, will you be prepared tomorrow? Tomorrow is still uncertain, and how do you know you will see a tomorrow?

2. What advantage is there in living a long life and, at the same time, to make so little progress? A long life does not always make us perfect; unfortunately, it often increases our guilt. If we could only point to a single day well lived! We count the anniversaries since our conversion to God, and they are many, but we have so little to show for them.

If dying is a frightful thing, perhaps, it is even more frightful to live a long time. Blessed is he who has the hour of death always before his eyes and daily prepares for it.[2] Have you ever seen anyone die? You too will travel that same road![3]

3. When you rise in the morning, think that you will not see evening; and when evening comes, do not be too certain that you will rise in the morning. *Be always ready,*[4] therefore, and so live that death may not find you unprepared. For many, death comes suddenly and unexpectedly; *The Son of Man is coming at an hour you do not expect.*[5] When your final hour arrives you will view your past life very differently, and your sorrow will be great for having been so easygoing and lackadaisical.

4. Wise and blessed is he who, during life, strives to be what he would like to be when death finds him. Yes, you can be assured of a happy death if you wholeheartedly despise the world, earnestly desire to advance in virtue, love discipline, dwell in repentance, show prompt obedience, exercise self-denial, and patiently bear all trials for the love of Christ.

[2]Cf. Sir. 7:36 [3]Cf. Sir. 38:22 [4]Luke 21:36
[5]Matt. 24:44

While you enjoy good health you can perform many good works, but when you are ill, I know not how many you will be able to do. Few men gain by being sick, just as few pilgrims become saints by frequently taking to the roads.

5. Do not postpone your soul's salvation to a later date, nor depend on your friends and neighbors, for they will forget you sooner than you think. It is better to make provision during your own lifetime by sending some good works ahead of you, than to count on another's help after your death. If you show no solicitude about yourself today, who will care about you later on? The present time is invaluable; *behold, now is the acceptable time; behold, now is the day of salvation.*[6]

Too bad that you are not making the best use of your life, for you could be gaining eternal life. The time will come when you wish you had a single day, or even an hour, to put yourself in order, but I honestly cannot say whether that day or hour will be given to you.

6. Listen! You can free yourself from the danger of an unprovided death, and you can deliver yourself from so frightening a terror. How? Always think of death! Live your present life in such a way that at death's hour you will be filled with joy and not overcome by panic. Die to the world now, and *you will later live with Christ.*[7] Despise the world now, and you will later go to Christ free of all the world's entangling chains. Bring your body into subjection by penance now, and in the end you will feel assured.

7. You fool! Why count on living a long time when you have no guarantee that you will live a single day more? Many presumed they would have a long life, but oh, how deceived they were, for how abruptly they were taken from this earth.

[6]2 Cor. 6:2 [7]Rom. 6:8

You have frequently heard it said that some individual was killed by the sword, or that another drowned, or that a third, falling from a great height, broke his neck, or still another choked while eating, or that someone met his death playing some game or other.

Everyone meets death.[8] Some die by fire and some by the sword; some by the plague and some at the hands of robbers. In the end, every *man's life vanishes as quickly as does a shadow.*[9]

8. Who will remember you when you are dead, and who will pray for you? Hence, my friend, do now all that you can, for you know not when you will die, nor what your eternal lot will be. While you have the time, *gather an everlasting treasure*[10] for yourself; let salvation be your only thought, and the things of God your only concern. And win friends for yourself among God's saints, honoring them and imitating their deeds so that when you do leave this life *they may receive you in the eternal habitations.*[11]

9. Live as becomes a *pilgrim and a stranger on earth,*[12] unconcerned about the world's cares, and keep your heart free and raised to God for this earth of ours *is no lasting city.*[13] Daily send your prayers, tears, and sighs heavenwards, asking that after death your soul may worthily and happily be united to Our Lord. Amen.

24. *Judgment and Punishment for Sins*

Keep your goal always before you and, remember, *you shall stand before a strict Judge,*[1] who knows all things, who accepts

[8] Eccles. 7:2 [9] Ps. 144:4 [10] Luke 12:33 [11] Luke 16:9
[12] 1 Pet. 2:11 [13] Heb. 13:14 [1] Rom. 14:10

no bribes, allows no excuses, and always passes a just judgment.

O foolish, wretched sinner! You sometimes become terrified when you see the face of an angry man, but *what answer will you give to God,*[2] who knows your every wicked deed? Prepare yourself for Judgment Day, for when it comes, you will not have a defense attorney to make excuses for you, but you will have to answer for yourself. Right now your efforts can bear profit, and your tears find acceptance; your sighs can be heard, and your sorrow find cleansing forgiveness.

2. The man who habitually exercises patience goes through a wholesome purgatory while still alive. He suffers injuries at the hands of others, but he is more concerned about their sin than his hurt. He willingly prays for those who harm him, wholeheartedly forgives offenses committed against him, and never puts off asking another's pardon. In fact, he more readily gives in to compassion than to anger. Too, he does not pamper his body, but by penances strives to bring it into complete subjection to his spirit.

It is better to purge our sins and root out our vices now, than to keep them for some future purgation. We certainly deceive ourselves by the obsessive love we have for our bodies!

3. What else does this fire have to feed on but your sins? The more lenient you are on yourself and the more you yield to your flesh, the greater will be your future suffering, for you are only storing up fuel for the fire.

There, a man will be punished according to the types of sins he committed. Those who are lazy will be pricked with red-hot spurs, and the glutton will be tormented by acute hunger and thirst. Those filled with lust and who have

[2]Job 31:14

indulged their senses will howl in pain like mad dogs.

4. There is no vice that will not have its own special torment. The proud will be filled with disgrace and humiliation, and the miserly will suffer all kinds of privations. One hour of suffering there will be more fierce than a hundred years spent performing the hardest of penances. For the damned there is neither rest nor comfort, but here we do enjoy a break from our toil and find comfort in our friends.

Therefore, take care and be sorry for your sins, that on Judgment Day you may be safe and numbered among the blessed. *Then the righteous man will stand in great confidence in the presence of those who have afflicted him.*[3] The man who now humbly submits to other men's judgments will then rise to judge; and the poor and humble will be wrapped in assurance, while the proud will be enveloped in fear.

5. He who learned *to be a fool for Christ*[4] and was despised by men will then be *revealed as truly wise.*[5] All trials patiently endured will prove a delight, while the throats of the wicked will be choked in sorrow. All the devout will rejoice and all the wicked will weep.

Mortified flesh will then exult more than if it had been brought up on the choicest of foods. Rough garments will take on brilliance, while silks and satins will lose their sheen. The humble hut will be esteemed more than any gold-encrusted palace. Steadfast patience will prove more valuable than all the world's power, and simple obedience will be more honored than worldly wisdom.

6. A good and pure conscience will then give you more joy than all the philosophy you have ever learned. The contempt for riches will weigh more than all the treasures in this world,

[3]Wis. 5:1 [4]1 Cor. 4:10 [5]*Ibid.*

and a fervent prayer will bring you more happiness than a multi-course banquet.

The silence you kept will then be more exhilarating than the telling of long tales, and holy deeds will be of greater value than nice-sounding words. And a strict life with hard penances will then bring you more pleasure than any worldly delight.

Remember, the sufferings you now bear are somewhat slight, but they will free you from greater sufferings in the future. Try and endure, here and now, what you will have to suffer later on! If now you can only put up with so little, how will you bear a punishment that is eternal? If a modicum of suffering now makes you uneasy, what will hell's fire do to you?

It is impossible for you to enjoy a double paradise: one here, based on the delights of this world, and the other reigning with Christ in His kingdom.

7. If, up to now, you have always lived amid honors and pleasures, what good would all this do you if you were to die this instant? All is vanity, therefore, except loving God and serving only Him. If you love God with your whole heart, you will fear neither death nor punishment, neither judgment nor hell. Perfect love opens up an unerring way to God. If, however, you still find delight in sin, then it is no wonder that you fear death and judgment.

If love cannot draw you away from evil then, at least, let the fear of hell pull you away. If you put off fearing God you cannot long persevere in goodness, but all too quickly, *you will fall into the devil's snares.*[6]

[6] 1 Tim. 6:9

25. *Earnestness in Amending Our Lives*

Be diligent and wide awake[1] in serving God, and keep in mind why you left the world and entered the monastery. Did you not come here to live for God and to become a holy and prayerful man? Therefore, seek perfection with a steady eagerness, for you will receive, within a brief space, *the reward of your labors*[2] and then both fear and sorrow will be foreign to you. Your labor is rather slight and yet you will find great and everlasting joy.

If you remain faithful and fervent in good works, *God will, without doubt, be faithful and generous in rewarding you*[3] And you must hold on tightly to your firm hope of attaining that reward, but do not give in to overconfidence; otherwise, you may become conceited and lazy.

2. Once there was a man given to much worrying, who wavered between hope and fear about his eternal salvation. One day, when quite depressed, he took himself to church and knelt down and prayed before one of the altars. This was the thought that ran through his mind: "If I could only be sure that I would persevere to the end." And immediately he heard heaven's answer within him: "If you did know this, what would you do? Well, then, do now what you would then do, and all will be well with you." Finding comfort in this answer, he gave himself totally to God's will and, thereafter, his anxiety and unsettledness came to an end. He was no longer interested in asking what his future would be, but he set himself *to learn God's holy will*[4] and pleasure whenever he was beginning or completing some good work.

[1]Rev. 3:2 [2]1 Cor. 3:8 [3]Sir. 51:30 [4]Rom. 12:2

3. The Prophet says: *Hope in the Lord, and do good, so that you will dwell in the land, and enjoy security.*[5] Many of us are kept back from spiritual progress and amendment of life because we fear the difficulties we are sure to meet and the effort it will cost us to overcome them. Nevertheless, the one who makes progress in the spiritual life is the very one who vigorously and strenuously strives to overcome these seemingly impossible obstacles. Both profit and merit are greater when we overcome ourselves and subject our will to our spirit.

4. All men do not have the same obstacles to overcome nor the same passions to be regulated, but he who is diligent and zealous — though he may have many strong passions — is better able to conquer them and achieve spiritual advancement than he who is easygoing and bending in his pursuit of virtue.

Two things are especially helpful in achieving amendment of life, namely, tear yourself forcibly from everything toward which human nature blindly and obsessively inclines, and seriously seek the virtues you especially need. Also take care to avoid or conquer those failings that often displease you in others.

5. Take advantage of everything that will help your progress, and if you see or hear of a good example, be on fire to imitate it. On the other hand, if you see something reprehensible, then do not imitate it, but avoid it. And if you have ever imitated such a deed, then correct it as soon as you can. Just as you take notice of the actions of others, be assured, they also notice yours.

How happy and agreeable it is to see a group of brothers, all fervent and devout, living a well-disciplined and well-ordered life.[6]

[5]Ps. 37:3 [6]Ps. 133:1

But how sad and distressing it is to see those who walk where they should not, and leave their rule unfulfilled. It is most harmful to set aside our order's goal, for which it was especially founded, and engage in matters in which you have no business.

6. Keep in mind your purpose in coming here and keep the Crucified Lord before your eyes. You certainly should feel ashamed if, after meditating on the life of Christ and after having been so many years following in His footsteps, you still have not conformed your life to His.

The religious who meditates devoutly on the most holy life and passion of Our Lord will find all that he needs to make his life worthwhile. In fact, he has no need to go beyond Jesus for he will discover nothing better. If Jesus Crucified would come into our hearts, how quickly and perfectly we would be instructed in the spiritual life.

7. The fervent religious willingly accepts and bears all that is commanded him. The lax and lukewarm religious faces problem after problem and suffers great anguish on every side, because he lacks the internal spiritual strength to comfort himself, and is forbidden, at the same time, to seek consolation outside him. The religious who avoids keeping his rule leaves himself open to grave ruin, and he who seeks ease and greater laxity will always be in trouble since there will always be something to displease him.

8. How then do the other countless religious get along who are strictly bound by the rule of cloister? They rarely go out and they live a retired life; their diet is poor and the habit they wear is coarse; their hours of labor are long and they speak very little; they extend their vigils late into the night and they rise early. They spend a great deal of time in prayer and in

reading, but in all things, these religious always keep themselves under discipline.

Think of the Carthusians, the Cistercians, and the monks and religious of the different religious orders who rise in the night to sing the Lord's praises. Shame on you for growing lazy in so holy an exercise, choosing to remain in bed while other religious are rising to praise God!

9. Would that we had no need to eat, drink, or sleep, but might always praise God and spend all our time only in spiritual pursuits. We would be much happier than we now are in our need to satisfy the demands of our human body. Would that there were no such demands, but only the spiritual nourishment of the soul, which, unfortunately, it rarely has a chance to taste!

10. When a man reaches the point where he no longer seeks consolation in any creature, then he enjoys his first taste of God and will be content with whatever comes to him. He will neither rejoice at having too much, nor will he be sorry at having too little, but he confidently rests in God, *who is all in all*[7] to him, and knows that with God nothing perishes or dies, but everything lives to Him and obeys His least word with prompt obedience.

11. *Keep your goal before you*[8] and remember that lost time never returns. Only by careful diligence will you acquire virtue. If you begin to grow lukewarm, you will become spiritually ill; but if you see that you grow in ardor, you will find great peace and your labors will grow lighter, all because of God's grace and your love of virtue.

The fervent and diligent man is ready for anything that happens. It takes harder work to eradicate faults and subdue

[7]Col. 3:11 [8]Sir. 7:36

passions than to engage in strenuous physical labor. If you do absolutely nothing about your small faults, you will, little by little, fall into greater ones. If you spend your day profitably, then your evening will be enjoyable. Watch over yourself, admonish yourself, and spur yourself onwards, and no matter what happens to others, never neglect your spiritual welfare. Your progress in the spiritual life is in direct proportion to the punishment you choose to inflict upon yourself.

BOOK II
Directives for the Interior Life

1. The Interior Life

The kingdom of God is within you,[1] says the Lord. If you *turn to the Lord with your whole heart*[2] and forsake this wretched world *your soul will find rest.*[3] Learn to despise everything outside you and give yourself to the inner life and you will see the kingdom of God coming within you. *The kingdom of God is living peacefully and joyfully in the Holy Spirit*[4] and this is not granted to the wicked. Christ will come and offer you His consolation if you will only prepare a suitable dwelling place within you.

Christ's glory and beauty are interiorly experienced and it is within you that He delights to be. He frequently visits the man who loves the interior life; He gently speaks to him, lovingly comforts him, gives him deep peace, and shares an intimacy beyond words.

2. Faithful soul, prepare your heart for its spouse that He may come and dwell within you. He says: *If a man loves Me, he will keep My word . . . and We will come to him and make Our home with him.*[5] Make room for Christ and deny entrance to everything else. *When you have Christ within you, you are rich*[6] and Christ is all you need. He will provide for you and faithfully supply you with all your needs, and you will not have to depend on men. Men are fickle, remember, and change quite quickly, and even more quickly do they disappoint you; but *Christ abides forever*[7] and stands firmly beside you unto the end.

[1]Luke 17:21 [2]Joel 2:12 [3]Matt. 11:29 [4]Rom. 14:17
[5]John 14:23 [6]1 Cor. 1:5 [7]John 12:34

3. We ought not place great trust in men; they are, after all, mortal and all too frail — though at times we do find them helpful and dear to us. Nor should we be overly disturbed if they sometimes disagree with us or even act against us. Today our friends, tomorrow our enemies; and vice versa. Men are as changeable as the wind!

Put all your trust in God[8] and let Him be your only love and fear only Him. He will defend you and do what is best for you. You have *no lasting city here,*[9] and wherever you may be you are always a *foreigner and a pilgrim,*[10] and you will have no rest until you are intimately united to Christ.

4. Why look about you? This place is not the place of your rest. *Your dwelling place is to be in heaven*[11] and you should view all earthly things as passing shadows. *Everything is transitory*[12] and so are you. So, do not cling to ephemeral things, otherwise, you will get caught in their webs and perish.

Let your every thought be on God the Most High, and *let your prayers be unceasing*[13] and directed to Christ. If you do not know how to meditate on sublime and heavenly things, then find repose in Christ's passion and gladly dwell in His sacred wounds. If you devoutly seek refuge in Jesus' wounds — those priceless signs of our salvation — you will feel great comfort in time of trial and you will learn not to care when men despise you. Instead you will easily bear whatever slander and vilification they cast upon you.

5. When Christ was among us in this world, He too was despised by men, and during His greatest need on the cross He was abandoned by friends and acquaintances and left to suffer insults alone. Christ chose to suffer and to be despised, and

[8]Prov. 3:5 [9]Heb. 13:14 [10]Heb. 11:13 [11]Phil. 3:20
[12]Wis. 5:9 [13]1 Thes. 5:17

you dare to complain if someone insults you? Christ had His enemies and His slanderers, and you want everyone to be your friend and benefactor? How will your patience[14] receive its crown if no trial ever comes your way? If you want to live a life free of all opposition, how will you be a friend of Christ? *If you desire to reign with Christ then suffer with Christ and for Christ.*[15]

6. If you have but once perfectly entered Jesus' heart and tasted a little of His burning love, you would then totally disregard personal comfort or discomfort, and would rejoice in the reproaches heaped upon you. If you love Jesus you will despise yourself. The true lover of Jesus and of truth is an inward man, and because he is free of all disordered affection he can freely turn to God and rise above himself in spirit to joyfully rest in Him.

7. He who sees all things as they really are and not as they are said to be or thought to be, is truly wise, *for God is his teacher*[16] and not man. He who knows how to walk with the light from within and make little of all outward things, needs no special place nor definite time to perform his religious exercises.

The interior man recollects himself quickly because he never wholly pours himself out on external things. Physical labor is no obstacle to him nor any other necessary occupation, but he accommodates himself to everything that comes his way. Since he is well disposed and well ordered within he

[14]When Thomas uses the word "patience," he means the virtue of patience, that is, suffering present evils in such a way as not to allow ourselves to be too much saddened by them. We not only grin and bear these trials, but we carry our cross with joy, or at least with resignation.

[15]2 Tim.2:12 [16]Is. 54:13

does not concern himself with the strange and unusual doings of men. To the degree that a man is drawn to exterior things, to that degree he becomes distracted and is thus hindered in the pursuit of the interior life.

8. If all were well with you and your soul purified, everything *would turn to your benefit*[17] and profit. The fact that many things often displease and disturb you is because you are not yet perfectly dead to yourself, nor have you cut yourself off from the things of this world. Nothing so stains and entangles a man's heart as the impure love of creatures. If you turn your back on all outward consolation you will be able to contemplate heavenly things and you will often exult in them.

2. *Humble Submission*

Do not worry about *who is for you or who is against you;*[1] rather see that God is with you in all that you do. If you have a clear conscience God will defend you, and whomever God chooses to help no man's malice can harm. If you suffer in calm silence you will, without doubt, experience God's help, and *since He alone knows the hour*[2] and the manner of your deliverance, place yourself in His hands. Truly, God desires to help you and to rescue you from your troubles. Many a time it is to our benefit if others know our defects and even reproach us because of them for they thus help us remain humble.

2. When a man humbles himself because of his faults, he readily becomes pleasing to others and reconciles himself to those he has offended. God protects and defends the humble

[17]Rom. 8:28 [1]Rom. 8:31 [2]Acts 1:7 [3]2 Cor. 7:6

man; *He loves and comforts him.*[3] *God favors the humble man, showers His abundant grace upon him,*[4] and after he has been brought low raises him up to glory.

To the humble man God reveals His secrets[5] and sweetly draws and invites him to Himself. Even after having accepted his shame the humble man lives in peace for he relies on God and not on the world's opinion. You will make no progress in the interior life until you regard yourself as lower than everyone else.

3. *The Man Who Loves Peace*

First, have peace within yourself, then you will be able to bring peace to others. The man of peace can achieve more good than the man who has great learning. The man of blind passion even turns good into evil and is quick to believe evil of others. The good and peace-loving man, on the other hand, turns everything into good.

The man who dwells in perfect peace suspects evil of no one. The man who is discontented and disgruntled has a heart filled with suspicion; he himself has no rest nor does he allow others to possess it. He often says what he ought not to say and omits saying what he should say. He thinks about another's obligations but dismisses his own. Therefore, first exercise your zeal upon yourself and only afterwards may you justly exercise it on your neighbor.

2. You are quite adept at excusing yourself and covering up your actions but yet you refuse to hear the excuses of others. It would be much more just for you to accuse yourself and to

[4]1 Pet. 5:5; James 4:6 [5]Matt. 11:25

excuse your brothers. If you wish others to put up with you, *you must learn to put up with others.*[1]

True charity and humility only know how to become angry with one's self and not with another. That's how far you are from possessing these virtues! It is no great accomplishment for you to live with those who are meek and good for this is something naturally pleasing to everyone. Everyone enjoys living in peace and love with those who think the same as they do, but if you can live in peace with those who are difficult, obdurate, and undisciplined, ah, that is a great grace, a manly and praiseworthy deed.

3. There are those who are at peace with themselves and *at peace with others*;[2] and there are those who have no peace and do not allow anyone else to be in peace. Indeed, these individuals are a burden to others but they are a heavier burden to themselves. Furthermore, there are those who not only have peace in themselves but also try to foster peace among others.

All our peace in this wretched world comes from our humble endurance of suffering and not from living a life without it. He who best knows how to suffer enjoys the greatest peace, and such a man is victor over himself, master of the world, friend of Christ, and heir of heaven.

4. *Simplicity of Purpose and Purity of Mind*

A man can lift himself above earthly cares by means of two wings, namely, by simplicity and purity.[1] This is a simplicity

[1]Eph. 4:2; Gal. 6:2 [2]Rom. 12:18

[1]Cf. Bernard, *On Consideration* V, 3

in our purpose and a purity in our affections. Simplicity looks to God, but purity finds Him and enjoys Him.

If you are interiorly free of all uncontrolled affections good actions will never be difficult for you, and if you desire and seek nothing other than God's good pleasure and your neighbor's welfare you shall enjoy interior freedom.

If your heart is right, then every creature is a mirror of life to you and a book of holy learning, for there is no creature — no matter how tiny or how lowly — that does not reveal God's goodness.

2. If you are interiorly good and pure you will perceive everything without difficulty and understand it correctly. A pure heart penetrates both heaven and hell.

As a man is within, so he judges what is outside him. If there be any joy in the world, certainly, the man of pure heart possesses it, and *if anywhere there be trials and tribulations,*[2] surely, it is the evil conscience that experiences them.

3. As iron in fire loses its rust and takes on a flaming glow, so the man who turns wholly to God loses his sluggishness and becomes a new man. When a man begins to grow lukewarm in spiritual matters, he fears the least labor and cheerfully accepts consolation from the outside world. But when he begins to overcome himself and walk manfully in the way of God, he takes little account of the things that were formerly burdensome to him.

[2]Rom. 2:9

5. The Need To Look at One's Self

We ought not place too much trust in ourselves because we are often without grace and understanding, and whatever little glimmer of understanding we do have we quickly extinguish by our negligence. We are so full of blindness that many times we are unaware of it. For example: we do an evil deed and to make things worse we make excuses for ourselves; or we act through passion and we call it zeal. Likewise, we reproach others for their petty faults but *we glide over our own glaring defects,*[1] or we are quick to notice and love to dwell on the affronts we suffer from others, but pay no attention to those we ourselves inflict. If a man justly and properly weighed his own actions he would never render a harsh judgment against another man.

2. The interior man places his spiritual welfare before everything else, and because he diligently attends to himself he does not gossip about the actions of others. You will only arrive at a devout inner life by watching over yourself and by being silent with regard to others.

If your total concern is God and your own spiritual welfare you will little note what happens outside you. When you are not attending to yourself what are you doing? If you have scurried about meddling in all sorts of things, *what good has all this done you if you have neglected your soul's welfare*?[2] If you wish to enjoy true peace and perfect union with God you must set all things aside and keep your eyes only upon yourself.

3. You will make great spiritual progress if you free yourself of all temporal cares but, on the other hand, you will fail miserably if you value and esteem anything that is worldly.

[1]Matt. 7:3 [2]Matt. 16:26

Let nothing be considered great or important to you, nothing pleasing or acceptable to you, except God and those things that come from Him. Regard all consolation coming from creatures as empty joys.

The soul that loves God despises everything that is not God. God alone, eternal and immeasurably great, *who fills all things*[3] with His goodness, is our soul's only comfort and our heart's true joy.

6. *The Joy of a Good Conscience*

The glory of the good man lies in the approval he receives from his good conscience.[1] If you have a good conscience you will always have joy within you. A clear conscience can bear a great deal *and though you may suffer adversity it still brings gladness to your heart.*[2] An evil conscience, on the other hand, is always uneasy and apprehensive. You will rest peacefully *if your heart has nothing against you.*[3] Rejoice only when you have done well.

The wicked never have true joy and never experience interior peace, for the Lord has said: *There is no peace for the wicked.*[4] And if they should tell you: "We are at peace for *no evil shall come upon us*[5] and no one dares to harm us," do not believe them for God's anger shall rise up, all of a sudden, and their deeds shall be reduced to nothing and *their plans brought to frustration.*[6]

2. It is not difficult for one who truly loves Jesus to glory in tribulation for this is *to glory in Our Lord's cross.*[7] Short-lived is the glory that exists among men for this kind of glory is always

[3]Jer. 23:24 [1]2 Cor. 1:12 [2]2 Cor. 7:4 [3]1 John 3:21
[4]Is. 48:22 [5]Mic. 3:11 [6]Ps. 146:4 [7]Gal. 6:14

mixed with sorrow. The good man's glory comes from his conscience and not from men's lips. The joy of the just man comes from God and is in God, and he rejoices because he possesses the truth.

Whoever desires true and everlasting glory cares not for what is temporal, and whoever seeks temporal glory does not despise the world as he should but shows little love for the glory of heaven. The man who is not affected by praise or blame enjoys great serenity of heart.

3. The man whose conscience is pure easily finds peace and contentment. You do not grow in holiness because of the praise you receive, nor do you become evil because of the blame poured upon you.

You are what you are and you cannot be said to be greater than what God knows you to be. If you rightly recognize what you really are you will not care what men say about you. After all, *men only see your face, but it is God who sees your heart.*[8] Men judge according to external deeds but only God can weigh the motives behind them.

One of the signs of having a humble soul is that you always do your best and think very little of yourself. And to refuse all consolation coming from creatures is a sign of great purity and inward trust in God.

4. He who seeks no outside testimony on his own behalf shows that he is totally committed to God, for St. Paul writes: *It is not the man who commends himself that is accepted, but the man whom the Lord commends.*[9]

What does it mean to be an interior man? It means *to walk inwardly with God*[10] and not be bound down by any outside affection.

[8] 1 Sam. 16:7 [9] 2 Cor. 10:18 [10] Mic. 6:8

7. Loving Jesus Above All Else

Blessed is he who understands what it is to love Jesus and to despise himself for Jesus' sake. Jesus wants to be your only love and to be loved above all else; therefore, you must abandon all other beloveds for your one Beloved. The love of a creature is fickle and deceitful while the love of Jesus is faithful and enduring. He who clings to a creature will fall when that creature fades away, but he who embraces Jesus shall stand firm forever.

Love Jesus and keep Him as your friend. When all others forsake you He will not leave you nor will He allow you to perish on the last day. Whether you like it or not the day will come when you will find yourself separated from everyone and from everything.

2. Hold fast to Jesus both in life and in death and commit yourself to His steadfast love, for He alone can help you when all others fail. Your Beloved is such that He admits no rival; He wants your heart all to Himself and desires to reign there as a king on his own throne.

If you could free yourself from all creatures Jesus would gladly dwell within you.[1] If you have placed your trust in men rather than in Jesus you will find that it was almost all wasted. Do not trust nor lean on a reed that is shaken in the wind.[2] *All flesh is grass, and all its glory shall fade like the flower in the field.*[3]

3. If you only look upon men's outward appearance you will soon be deceived, and if you seek consolation and profit from them most often you will end up being the loser. If you seek Jesus in everything you will certainly find Him, and if you seek yourself you will surely find yourself, but to your

[1]Cf. John 15:4 [2]Cf. Matt. 11:7 [3]Is. 40:6

own disaster. You do yourself greater harm by not seeking Jesus than if the whole world and all your enemies were against you.

8. *Close Friends with Jesus*

When Jesus is present all is well and nothing seems arduous, but when He is absent everything becomes difficult. When Jesus does not speak within us we are without consolation, but when He does speak — even a single word — our consolation is great.

Did not Mary Magdalene immediately rise from the place where she was weeping when Martha said to her: *The Teacher is here and is calling for you*?[1] Happy that hour when Jesus calls us from tears to spiritual joy!

How dry and listless you are when Jesus is not with you! It is vain and foolish for you to desire anything other than Jesus. To lose Him is to suffer a greater loss than to lose the whole world.

2. What has the world to offer you without Jesus? To be without Jesus is a painful hell but to be with Him is a sweet paradise. *If Jesus is with you no enemy can harm you.*[2] Whoever finds Jesus discovers a wonderful treasure, a treasure above all others, and he who loses Jesus loses a great deal — more than the entire world. The man who lives without Jesus is the poorest of the poor, but he who has Jesus as his friend is the richest of men.

3. It is a great art to know how to live with Jesus, and to know how to keep His friendship demands great wisdom. Be

[1]John 11:28 [2]Cf. Rom. 8:31

humble and peace-loving and Jesus will be with you. Be devout and calm and Jesus will abide with you.

Should you, however, choose to return to worldly affairs you will quickly drive Jesus away and lose His grace, and if you do drive Him away and lose Him *to whom will you turn*?[3] Whom will you now seek as your friend? Without a friend you can hardly live your life, and if Jesus is not your friend above all friends then, indeed, you shall be sad and lonely.

You are a fool to place your trust in other men and to rejoice in them. You should be willing to have the whole world against you rather than offend Jesus. Of all those whom you hold dear, let Jesus alone be your most special friend.

4. Love everyone else for the sake of Jesus and love Jesus for His own sake. Jesus Christ alone deserves to be loved with an exclusive love for, of all our friends, He alone is truly good and faithful. Love your enemies as well as your friends, for Him and in Him, and pray they all may come to know and love Him.

On your part never desire to be exclusively loved or praised because such love belongs to God alone and *there is no one like Him*.[4] Neither desire that any one's heart be filled with love for you nor should your heart be filled with love for another, but let Jesus be within you and see Him in every good individual.

5. Be inwardly pure and free and remain separated from all creatures. If you wish rest and wish to see how sweet the Lord is you must bring to God a pure and uncluttered heart. You will never achieve this union *unless God's grace first draws you to Him*,[5] and after having disentangled yourself from all creatures you shall be united to Him — alone with Him who is alone.

When God's grace comes to a man he gains the necessary

[3]John 6:68 [4]Jer. 10:6 [5]John 6:44

strength to do all things, but when that grace leaves him he grows weak and enfeebled and feels as abandoned as a prisoner awaiting severe punishment.

Still, you must not become dejected nor give in to despair but calmly await God's will, and for the honor of Jesus Christ bear whatever comes your way. Remember, after winter comes the summer, after night comes the morning, and after the storm comes the great calm.

9. *Lacking All Consolation*

It is not difficult to despise human consolation while you are enjoying divine consolation.[1] But it is great and wonderful to be able to do without all consolation, both human and divine, and for God's honor gladly endure the heart's interior exile and not seek one's self nor think of one's deserts.

Is there anything exceptional in being happy and feeling devout when God's grace touches you? Everybody looks forward to such a time. The man who is carried along by God's grace indeed rides smoothly and it is no wonder that he feels no drag since he is supported by the Almighty and led by the Supreme Guide.

2. We would all like to enjoy some consolation and it is difficult for a man to strip himself so completely. The holy martyr Lawrence, with his priest, overcame the world because he despised all that appeared delightful in the world, and for

[1]Consolation is a gift of the Holy Spirit that produces delight, peace, and quiet in the soul. It arouses the soul to greater faith, hope and love, and instills the desire for heavenly realities and for the practice of virtue and in the time of suffering it offers support and encouragement. The opposite of consolation is desolation.

the love of Christ calmly suffered Sixtus, God's High Priest and whom he especially loved, to be taken from him.[2] Lawrence's love for his Creator surpassed his love for Sixtus and he preferred God's good pleasure to that of human consolation.

You too must learn to part with some close and beloved friend for the love of God, and when a friend gives you up do not take it too badly for you know that eventually we all must be separated from one another.

3. Before a man learns to fully master himself and to direct all his affection toward God he must first undergo a hard and long struggle within himself. When a man relies on himself he easily turns to human consolation; but the man who truly loves Christ and diligently pursues virtue neither looks for human consolation nor seeks any such sensible pleasure, but prefers hard trials and is willing to undertake severe labors for Christ.

4. When God gives you some spiritual consolation accept it with thanksgiving and realize that it is a gift from God and not due you because of any merit on your part. So, do not yield to pride, nor be overly joyous, nor foolishly give in to presumption; rather, that gift of consolation should make you more humble, more prudent, and more cautious in your actions for your hour of joy will pass and temptation will follow in its place.

And when consolation does leave you do not give up hope immediately, but with patient humility wait for a visit from on high for God is able to give you a still greater consolation in its place. To those who have experienced the ways of God this manner of acting is neither new nor strange for the great saints

[2]The Roman deacon, Lawrence, was martyred four days after Pope Sixtus II met his death, probably in A.D. 258.

and ancient prophets have often experienced such exchanges.

5. When the Psalmist experienced grace within himself he said, *In my abundance I shall never be moved,*[3] but when that grace was withdrawn he experienced a different feeling and said, *You have turned Your face from me and I was dismayed.*[4] Still the Psalmist did not despair but prayed the more earnestly to God saying: *To You, O Lord, I will cry out and to my God I will make my prayer.*[5] Finally, when he obtains his request he testifies that his prayer has been answered: *The Lord has heard me and has had pity on me. The Lord has become my helper.*[6] What did the Lord do? *You have changed my mourning into joy and have surrounded me with gladness.*[7]

If this is the way God has dealt with great saints then we poor weaklings ought not to be discouraged if we sometimes find ourselves fervent and at other times frigid. This is due to the Spirit who comes and goes according to His own good pleasure. Thus, holy Job says: *You visited him early in the morning and suddenly You tested him.*[8]

6. What other foundation can there be for my hope or in whom ought I to confide, except in God's great mercy and in the sole hope of heavenly grace? It does not matter whether I have good men or devout brethren or faithful friends standing at my side, or whether I am carrying holy and fine treatises with me, or sing pleasing chants and hymns, for all these are of little help and afford me little pleasure when grace has departed from me and I am left alone in my poverty. For times such as these there is no better remedy than patient abandonment of myself to God's will.

7. I have never encountered anyone, no matter how devout

[3]Ps. 30:6 [4]Ps. 30:7 [5]Ps. 30:8 [6]Ps. 30:10
[7]Ps. 30:11 [8]Job 7:18

and religious, who did not sometimes experience a withdrawal of grace or a decrease in devotion. No saint has ever been so enraptured or so illumined as not to have had temptations sooner or later. The man who has not been tested by some trial for God's sake is not worthy of the sublime contemplation of God. Temptation is the usual sign that consolation will follow and heavenly consolation is promised to those who have been proven by temptation: *To him, who conquers,* Our Lord says, *I will grant to eat of the tree of life.*[9]

8. Divine consolation is given a man so that he may better be able to endure adversity, and the temptation that follows is to keep him from becoming proud about his good deeds. Since the devil does not sleep and since your flesh is not yet dead, never stop readying yourself for combat. Your enemy is on your right and on your left and is ever watching.

10. *Being Thankful for God's Grace*

Why do you seek rest when you were born to work?[1] Prepare yourself for patient suffering rather than for consolation, for bearing the cross rather than for rejoicing. Who is the man in this world who would not gladly welcome spiritual joy and consolation if he could always have them?

Spiritual consolation surpasses all worldly delights and bodily pleasures. The delights of this world are worthless and vile but those of the spirit are joyful and noble for they alone proceed from virtuous deeds and are infused by God into a pure heart. No man can always enjoy divine consolation no

[9]Rev. 2:7 [1]Cf. Job 5:7

matter how much he would like to — his time of temptation has not yet come to its end.

2. A false sense of liberty and overconfidence in one's self are obstacles to such heavenly visitations. God is indeed beneficent in granting the grace of consolation but it is man who does ill in neglecting to refer everything back to God with a grateful heart. As a result, God's grace does not flow into us because we are ungrateful to the giver and do not return everything to the source from which it came. Grace will always be granted the man who gives worthy thanks for graces received, and the graces that the humble man receives are usually those withheld from the man who is proud.

3. I do not want any consolation that would take away my repentance, nor do I seek any consolation that would lead me to pride. All that is sublime is not necessarily holy, nor is everything sweet a good thing. Every desire is not pure, nor is all that we hold dear pleasing to God. Rather, I am most happy to accept the grace that will make me more humble, more fearful, and more prompt to renounce myself.

The man who has been taught by the gift of grace and has learned by the pain of its withdrawal will not dare to attribute any good to himself but readily recognizes his naked poverty. *Give God what is God's*[2] and take to yourself what is yours, that is, thank God for His grace and take unto yourself the guilt of your sins and the punishment they deserve.

4. Always *take the lowest place for yourself*[3] and the highest will be given to you. There is a highest place only because there is a lowest.

The saints who are the greatest before God are the least in

[2]Matt. 22:21 [3]Luke 14:10

their own eyes, and the greater their glory the more humble are they in themselves. Because they are filled with truth and the glory of heaven they seek no empty glory, and because they are firmly established in God they can in no way yield to pride.

Men who attribute to God whatever good they have received do not seek glory from other men but *seek only the glory that comes from God.*[4] Their desire is that God be praised above all things, both in Himself and in all His saints, and this is their constant aim.

5. Be grateful, then, for even the least gift and you will be worthy of receiving greater ones. Consider the least gift as something great and look on it as something special. If you consider the dignity of the giver of these gifts then none of them will ever seem to you small or unimportant, for no gift coming from God on high can be called insignificant.

And if God should send you punishment and suffering, accept these too, for whatever God sends you He sends for your salvation. If you desire to persevere in God's grace, then, be thankful for the grace when it is given you and be patient when it is taken from you. Pray for its return and then be watchful and humble lest you lose it again.

11. *The Few Who Love the Cross of Jesus*

Jesus today has many lovers of His heavenly kingdom but few of them carry His cross. He has many friends who ask for consolation but few who pray for affliction. *He has many*

[4]John 5:44

companions to share His meals[1] but few to share His abstinence.

We all want to rejoice with Him but few of us are willing to suffer anything for His sake. Many follow Jesus up to the breaking of the bread but *few go on to the drinking of the chalice of His passion.*[2] Many admire His miracles but few follow in the ignominy of His cross.

Many love Jesus as long as adversity does not touch them and many praise and bless Him as long as they receive consolation from Him. But if He should hide Himself and leave them for even a brief period they begin to complain and fall into severe depression.

2. Those who love Jesus for Jesus' sake and not for any reason of their own, praise Him in every affliction and anguish of heart just as they do in moments of great consolation. And if in the future God should choose never to send them any consolation they would equally praise Him and be grateful to Him.

3. Powerful is that pure love for Jesus that is not tainted by self-love and has no admixture of self-interest. Those who are always looking for consolation are no better than mercenaries! Isn't this the word we should use to describe them? Don't those who continually seek their personal comfort and gain love themselves more than they love Christ? Where will we find a man willing to serve God without receiving something in return?

4. Rarely do you encounter someone who is so spiritual that he has completely divested himself of all things. Where will you find someone who is truly poor in spirit and totally detached from all creatures? He is *far more precious than jewels*[3] brought from distant shores.

[1]Sir. 6:10 [2]Matt. 20:22 [3]Prov. 31:10

If a man were to give up all his possessions it would be as nothing, and if he were to fulfill very heavy penances it would still not be enough. *If he possessed universal knowledge*[4] he would still be far from his goal, and if he possessed outstanding virtue and burned with extraordinary fervor, *he would still lack the one thing most necessary*[5] to him. And what is that? Having left all things behind he should renounce himself, abandon himself completely, keeping nothing of his self-love, and when he has done all that he knows must be done, then let him realize that he has done nothing.

5. He should not consider great what others esteem as great, rather he should truthfully admit that he is but a worthless servant. It is Truth Itself that teaches us: *When you have done all that was commanded you, say to yourselves, we are unworthy servants.*[6] Only then will he achieve poverty and nakedness of spirit and be able to say with the Prophet, *I am alone and poor.*[7] There is no one richer, nor one more powerful, nor one who enjoys greater freedom than the man who can renounce himself and his possessions and choose the lowest of places.

12. *The Royal Road of the Holy Cross*

Many think this a hard saying: *Deny yourself, take up your cross and follow Jesus;*[1] but it will be much harder to hear those final words: *Depart from me, you cursed ones, into everlasting fire.*[2] Those who now gladly listen to *the word of the cross*[3] and follow it *will not be in terror when they later hear that sentence of eternal damnation.*[4]

[4] 1 Cor. 13:2 [5] Luke 10:42 [6] Luke 17:10 [7] Ps. 25:16

[1] Matt. 16:24 [2] Matt. 25:41 [3] 1 Cor. 1:18 [4] Ps. 112:7

When the Lord comes in judgment this sign of the cross will be in the heavens[5] and all the servants of the cross who, in their lifetime, *conformed themselves to Jesus Crucified*[6] will approach Christ the Judge with full confidence.

2. Why do you then fear to carry the cross? This is the way that leads to the kingdom.

In the cross we have salvation;[7] in the cross we have life; in the cross we have protection from our enemies.

In the cross there is the inpouring of heavenly sweetness; in the cross there is the strengthening of minds; in the cross there is spiritual joy.

In the cross is the height of virtue; in the cross is the fullness of holiness.

In the cross alone do we find the soul's eternal salvation and hope of everlasting life. *Take up your cross, therefore, and follow Jesus*[8] *and you will pass into unending life.*[9]

Carrying His own cross Jesus[10] preceded you, and on the cross He died for you so that you too might bear your cross and long to die on it. *If you die with Him you shall also live with Him,*[11] and if you are His companion in suffering you shall likewise be His companion in glory.

3. Everything is founded on the cross and everything depends on our dying on the cross. There is no other way to life and interior peace except the holy way of the cross and our daily dying to self.

No matter where you walk or what you look for, you will

[5]The monastic office for Nones, for the Feast of the Exaltation of the Holy Cross, reads: "The sign of the cross shall be in the heavens when the Lord shall come to judge."

[6]Rom. 8:29 [7]Cf. Bernard, *Second Sermon for the Feast of St. Andrew.*

[8]Matt. 16:24 [9]Matt. 25:46 [10]John 19:17 [11]Rom 6:8

find no higher road above nor a safer road below than the road of the holy cross.

Plan as you will and arrange everything as seems best to you, still you will find some suffering in your life. Whether you wish it or not, you will always find the cross for you will either experience some pain in your body or perhaps have to endure some affliction of spirit in your soul.

4. Sometimes God may leave you to yourself and sometimes your neighbor will try you; but worse, you will often be a burden to yourself. There is no remedy to free you from this nor is there any ointment to ease the pain, but you must bear it as long as God wills.

God wants you to learn to endure affliction without relief, wholly to submit yourself to Him and to become more humble by passing through adversity.

No man's heart can experience what Christ endured in His passion except the man who suffers as He did.

The cross is, therefore, always in readiness for you and everywhere awaits you. Wherever you choose to run you will not escape it because you always take yourself with you and you will always find yourself.

Gaze upwards and downwards, look inside you and outside you and everywhere you will find the cross. If you desire internal peace and want to gain an everlasting crown then you must everywhere exercise patient resignation.

5. If you carry your cross willingly, it will carry you and lead you to your desired goal where suffering will be no more; but that will not be while you are here. If on the other hand you carry your cross grudgingly, then you turn it into a heavy burden weighing yourself down the more and still you must carry it. If you should throw off one cross you will surely find

another and perhaps one that is even heavier.

6. Do you think you can escape what no mortal has ever been able to avoid? Do you know of any saint who, during his life, was without the cross and some affliction? Even Our Lord Jesus Christ, while He lived on this earth, was not for a single hour without the pain of His passion. *It was fitting,* He said, *that the Christ should suffer and rise from the dead and so to enter into His glory.*[12] How is it that you seek a way that is different from that of the royal road, which alone is the road of the holy cross?

7. Christ's entire life was a cross and a martyrdom, and you look for rest and pleasure? You are mistaken, O, you are mistaken, if you seek anything other than affliction, for *our whole mortal life is full of misery*[13] and surrounded by crosses. The greater the height a man reaches in the spiritual life, the heavier he finds his cross, but this is only because the pain of being in exile from God is in proportion to his love of God.

8. This individual, though greatly afflicted in many ways, is still not without some consolation for he recognizes the great reward that will be his by bearing his cross. As long as he willingly carries it the weight of his affliction is changed into the certain knowledge that God will send His consolation. The more the flesh is worn away by affliction so much the more is the spirit strengthened by interior grace.

Sometimes an individual, because of his desire to be conformed to Christ's cross, is powerfully strengthened by his desire to suffer these trials and tribulations rather than to be without them. He firmly believes that the greater and the heavier the burden he suffers the more pleasing he is to God. It is Christ's grace and not man's power that can and does effect

[12]Luke 24:46 [13]Job 14:1

such wonderful things in our frail human flesh, enabling it to embrace with great spiritual fervor and love what it naturally abhors and avoids.

9. It is not according to man's nature to bear the cross and love it, to chastise the body and bring it into subjection, to avoid honors and be willing to suffer insults. It is not man's nature to despise one's self and to wish to be despised, to endure opposition and failure, or to desire no prosperity whatsoever in this world.

If you take a look at yourself you will realize that by yourself you can do none of these, but if you put your trust in the Lord He will send you strength from heaven empowering you to subject the world and the flesh to your holy desires. Nor will you fear the devil, your enemy, as long as you are dressed in the armor of faith and are signed with the cross of Christ.

10. Be determined then and, like a good and faithful servant, manfully carry the cross of Our Lord who was crucified out of love for you. Be ready to suffer many trials and much trouble in this wretched life for such will be your lot wherever you are, and you will find it to be so no matter where you may choose to hide.

It must be so, and there is no escaping such sorrows and sufferings except by bearing them with patience. *If you desire to be Christ's friend and to share with him,*[14] then drink lovingly of the chalice of the Lord. Leave all consolations to God to dispose of as He wills, but as for yourself, be ready to bear afflictions and look upon them as the greatest consolations. Even if you alone were to suffer all possible tribulations your suffering in this life would still bear no proportion to the glory

[14]John 13:8

that is to come, the glory that your suffering has earned for you.

11. When you have arrived at the point when affliction becomes something sweet and you regard it as a pleasure for the sake of Christ, then all is well with you and you have found paradise here on earth. But as long as suffering is something that vexes you and which you seek to avoid, then things will go ill with you, for the very affliction you are trying to escape will follow you wherever you go.

12. If you put your mind to doing what you have to do, that is, suffering and dying, then everything will go better for you and you will find peace. Even if you were caught up with St. Paul *into the third heaven*[15] that would be no guarantee that you were not to suffer further adversity. Jesus said: *I will show him how much he must suffer for My name's sake.*[16] Therefore, you still have to suffer if you wish to love Jesus and serve Him constantly.

13. Would that you were *worthy to suffer something for Jesus' name*![17] What glory would then be yours! How happy all the saints of God would be! How wonderfully you would nurture your neighbor's spiritual life! Indeed, all men praise suffering with patience but there are only a few who are actually willing to do it. With good reason, then, you should be willing to suffer a little for Christ when there are many who suffer far worse things to achieve worldly advancement.

14. Know for certain that you must lead a life constantly dying to yourself, and the *more you die to yourself the more you will live to God.*[18] No one can understand heavenly things unless he first resigns himself to bearing afflictions for Christ's sake.

[15]2 Cor. 12:2 [16]Acts 9:16 [17]Acts 5:41 [18]Rom. 6:8

Nothing is more acceptable to God, nor is there anything more beneficial in this world than being willing to suffer for Christ. If you were given the choice you ought to prefer to suffer adversity for Christ's sake rather than to be comforted by many consolations. In this way you make yourself more like Christ and model yourself more closely on the saints.

Merit and advancement in our state of life do not rest on sweet consolations but in bearing great trials and tribulations.

15. If there were anything better suited for and more useful to man's salvation than suffering, then Christ certainly would have pointed it out to us by His teaching and His example. Speaking to the disciples who followed Him and to those who desired to be His followers, Christ clearly urged them: *If any one will come after Me let him deny himself and take up his cross and follow Me.*[19]

After you have read this and seriously reflected upon it, this should be your conclusion: *it is fitting for us to enter into the kingdom of God through many afflictions.*[20]

[19]Luke 9:23; Mark 8:34; Matt. 16:24 [20]Acts 14:22

BOOK III
On Interior Consolation

1. *Christ Speaks Interiorly to the Faithful Soul*

I will listen to what the Lord God will say to me.[1] Blessed is the soul that *listens when the Lord speaks to it*[2] and receives consoling words from His lips.

Blessed are the ears that are attuned to *God's quiet whisper*[3] and ignore the world's raucous sounds. Blessed, indeed, are the ears that disregard the noises outside and wholly attend to the voice teaching truth within.

Blessed are the eyes that are closed to the outer world and are fixed on interior things. Blessed are they who discover these inward realities and try to prepare themselves by daily prayerful exercises to better understand the secrets of heaven.

Blessed are they who are wholly occupied with God and have shaken off the manacles of the world.

2. My soul, pay attention to these matters and close tightly the doors of your senses so that you may only hear what the Lord speaks to you.

Thus says your Beloved: "*I am your salvation,*[4] your peace, and your life. Keep close to Me and you shall find peace." Do not waste your time on temporal things but seek those that are eternal. What are temporal things if not deceitful illusions? Furthermore, what good are all creatures if the Creator has forsaken you? Once you have set aside all earthly things, make yourself pleasing to your Creator and be faithful to Him so that you may arrive at true happiness.

[1]Ps. 85:8 [2]1 Sam. 3:9 [3]1 Kings 19:12 [4]Ps. 35:3

2. *Truth Speaks within Us without the Strident Sound of Words*

Disciple:

Speak Lord, for Your servant is listening.[1] *I am Your servant; give me understanding that I may know Your decrees.*[2] *Incline my heart to the words of Your mouth*[3] and *let them come upon me as the dew.*[4]

In years gone by the children of Israel said to Moses: *Speak to us and we will listen, but do not let God speak to us or we shall die.*[5] In this manner I do not pray, O Lord, but like the prophet Samuel I humbly and sincerely beg: *Speak, Lord, for Your servant is listening.*[6]

Let not Moses or any other prophet speak to me, but rather You speak to me, O Lord God, who inspire and enlighten all prophets. You have no need of them for alone You can perfectly instruct me, but without You they can achieve nothing.

2. The prophets may indeed be able to sound the words but they cannot impart the spirit; their words may be pleasing to the ear but if You remain silent they do not enflame hearts.

The prophets pass on Your message but it is You who unlock its meaning; they proclaim Your mysteries but it is You who unfold their secrets. They teach Your commandments but You enable us to fulfill them; they point out the way to You but You give us the strength to walk upon it.

The prophets touch us only externally but You teach and enlighten our hearts; they outwardly apply the water but *You make the seed grow.*[7] They utter the words but You give understanding to what we hear.

[1] 1 Sam. 3:10 [2] Ps. 119:125 [3] Ps. 78:1 [4] Deut. 32:2
[5] Ex. 20:19 [6] 1 Sam. 3:10 [7] 1 Cor. 3:7

3. Let not Moses, then, speak to me, but You speak, my Lord God, eternal Truth, for if I am only outwardly admonished and not interiorly set on fire I may die and find that my life was without fruit, and at the moment of judgment I may be condemned for hearing the word but not fulfilling it, for knowing it but not loving it, for believing it but not living it.

Speak, then, Lord, for Your servant is listening;[8] *You have the words of eternal life.*[9] Speak to me and comfort my soul; help me to amend my whole life, and may it, in turn, give You praise, glory, and endless honor.

3. *Listening to God's Words with Humility*

Jesus:

My son, hear My words for they are exceptionally sweet and surpass those of the philosophers and wise men of the world. *My words are spirit and life*[1] and are not to be measured by human understanding. They are *to be listened to in silence*[2] and received with all humility and deep love, and you are not to use them in promoting yourself.

Disciple:

I answered: *Blessed is the man whom You instruct, O Lord, whom You teach by Your law and to whom You give rest in troublesome times,*[3] for no longer will he feel desolate on this earth of ours.

Jesus:

From the beginning I have instructed the prophets and even now I

[8]1 Sam. 3:10 [9]John 6:68
[1]John 6:63 [2]Eccles. 9:17 [3]Ps. 94:12-13

do not cease to speak[4] to all men, but many have closed their ears to Me and have hardened themselves against Me.

2. Most men are more eager to listen to the world than to God, and many are more inclined to follow the desires of their flesh than God's good pleasure.

The world promises things that are passing and of little value and it is served with great enthusiasm; I promise things that are most excellent and eternal and men's hearts remain indifferent. Do you know anyone who serves and obeys Me in all things with the same alacrity with which the world and its lords are served? *Be ashamed, O Sidon, says the sea.*[5] Would you like to know the reason? Then listen to this.

For a pittance men will travel a great distance, but for eternal life many will scarcely take a single step. They look ahead to puny gains and sometimes shamefully wrangle over a single penny; neither do they hesitate to wear themselves out working day and night for some foolish promise or trifling object.

3. But for the good that never changes, for the prize beyond all prizes, for the highest honor and the glory that never ends, men, alas, are too lazy to put forth the slightest effort. You should be ashamed, lazy and evergrumbling servant, when you see other men more eager to lose their souls than you are to gain life! They find greater joy in chasing after empty dreams than you have in pursuing the truth.

The desires of these men often end in disappointment but My promises never deceive anyone. The man who trusts in Me I never send away empty. When I make a promise I keep it, and I fulfill whatever I have pledged — if only you remain

[4]Heb. 1:1-2 [5]Is. 23:4

faithful to My love unto the end. I reward all good men and I heartily acclaim all who are devout.

4. Write My words in your heart and seriously reflect upon them for you will need them when temptation comes.

What you are now unable to understand as you read, you will come to know when I visit you. I usually visit My chosen friends in two ways: by testing them in temptation and by comforting them with consolation. And daily I offer them two lessons; in one I reproach them for their faults but in the other I encourage them to advance in virtue.

He who has My words and *casts them aside has a judge to judge him on the last day.*[6]

Disciple:

Prayer for the Grace of True Devotion

5. Lord, my God, You are all my good. Who am I *that I should dare speak to You?*[7] I am the least and poorest of Your servants, a wretched little worm, much poorer and more contemptible than I realize or dare to express.

Remember, Lord, *I am nothing,*[8] have nothing, and can do nothing. You alone are good, just, and holy. *You can do all things;*[9] You give all things; You fill all things. Only the sinner do You send away empty.

Remember Your mercies[10] and fill my heart with Your grace for You *do not wish Your works to be without their effects.*[11]

6. How can I endure myself and this wretched life unless You strengthen me with Your mercy and grace? *Turn not Your face from me,*[12] nor delay Your visit; take not Your consolation

[6]John 12:48 [7]Gen. 18:27 [8]2 Cor. 12:11 [9]Job 42:2
[10]Ps. 25:6 [11]Wis. 14:5 [12]Ps. 143:7

from me, otherwise, *my soul will become as the parched earth longing for water.*[13]

Lord, *teach me to do Your will;*[14] teach me to live worthily and humbly in Your presence. You, Lord, are my wisdom; You truly know me as I am, and have known me before the world came to be and before I came into being.

4. *Walking before God in Truth and Humility*

Jesus:

Son, *walk before Me in truth*[1] and always *seek Me with sincerity of heart.*[2] Whoever walks before Me in truth shall be protected from the assaults of the evil one, and the truth shall deliver him from all deceivers and from the lies of wicked men. If *the truth sets you free,*[3] then you are truly free and you need not concern yourself about other men's empty words.

Disciple:

Lord, what You say is true and so I ask You, let it be as You have said. *Let Your truth be my teacher*[4] and let it guard and preserve me until I come to my final saving end. Let Your truth free me from all evil affection and unregulated love so that I may walk with You with great freedom of heart.

Jesus:

2. I who am the Truth will teach you *what is right and pleasing in My sight.*[5]

[13]Ps. 143:6; Ps. 63:1 [14]Ps. 143:10 [1]Gen. 17:1 [2]Wis. 1:1
[3]John 8:32 [4]Ps. 25:5 [5]1 John 3:22

Recall your sins with deep sorrow and hatred, and never think of yourself as being in any way important because of any good you may have done. Indeed, you are a sinner and you are still subjected to and ensnared by your many passions. Left to yourself you always lean toward nothingness. You quickly fall and quickly you are overcome; you are quickly disturbed and quickly you become discouraged.

You have nothing in you in which you can glory but there is much in you for which you ought to humble yourself. You are much weaker than you think.

3. Therefore, of all the things you have accomplished, look upon none of them as being great. Let nothing appear important, outstanding, or extraordinary, and consider nothing lofty, sublime, or inestimable, except that which is eternal.

Let eternal Truth alone please you above all things and let your own worthlessness always displease you.

There is nothing you should fear more than your faults and your sins, and there is nothing you should hold in greater hatred or be more diligent in avoiding. Your faults and sins should cause you more displeasure than if you were to lose all earthly goods.

Some men *walk before Me but they are not sincere.*[6] Impelled by some arrogant curiosity of theirs, they strive to know My secrets and to penetrate the sublime realities of God while, at the same time, they neglect themselves and their salvation. They are filled with pride and conceit, and because I resist them they frequently fall into serious temptation and grave sin.

4. *Fear God's judgment*[7] and tremble before *the Almighty's anger.*[8] Do not presume to investigate minutely into the

[6]Tob. 3:5 [7]Ps. 119:120 [8]2 Macc. 7:38

workings of the Most High;[9] rather, closely examine your own misdeeds, in how many things you have given offense and how much good you have neglected to do.

Some individuals confine their devotion to the pages in their prayerbooks, while others confine it to holy pictures or statues or some external sign. There are those who *have Me on their lips but have little of Me in their hearts.*[10]

On the other hand, there are some who, because they are enlightened in mind and are purified in affection, always yearn for eternal things. They prefer not to hear about earthly matters and deeply grieve over the fact that they are subject to the demands of human nature. They are keenly aware of what *the Spirit of Truth speaks within them,*[11] as It teaches them to despise terrestrial things and to long for celestial realities, to set this world aside and to aspire day and night for heaven.

5. *The Wonderful Effects of Divine Love*

Disciple:

Heavenly Father, Father of my Lord Jesus Christ, I bless You since You have deigned to be mindful of me, poor as I am. *Father of mercies and God of all comfort,*[1] I give You thanks for at times refreshing me with Your consolation, undeserving as I am of any and all such gifts. To You, Father, together with Your only-begotten Son, and the Holy Spirit, the Comforter, I offer praise and glory, now and for ever.

Lord God, my holy Lover, when You enter my heart everything rejoices within me. *You are my glory*[2] and *the joy of*

[9]Cf. Sir. 11:4 [10]Is. 29:13 [11]Matt. 10:20
[1]2 Cor. 1:3 [2]Ps. 3:3

my heart;[3] You are my hope and *my refuge in the day of my distress.*[4]

2. Because my love is still weak and my virtue still unsure, I especially need Your strength and comfort. Come to me more often and teach me Your holy ways. Free me from my evil passions and heal my heart of all disordered love so that once I am interiorly healed and purified I may become more ready to love You, stronger to endure suffering for You, and more steadfast in persevering in You.

3. Love is something great and truly magnificent. *Love alone makes burdens light*[5] and makes uneven loads seem equal. Love carries its heavy burden without feeling burdened and transforms its bitterness into something sweet and savory. The love of Jesus is noble and urges us to perform great deeds and excites us to always desire what is more perfect.

Love wishes to soar to the heights and does not want to be tied down here below. Love wants to fly freely, clear of all earthly attachments, lest its interior vision become dim, clouded by temporal affairs, and eventually succumb under their heavy weight.

There is nothing sweeter than love, nothing stronger, nothing more sublime, more robust, nor better in heaven or on earth; this *love comes from God*[6] and finds its rest only in Him who is above everything else.

4. The man in love flies high, runs swiftly, and overflows with joy. He is totally free for there is nothing to hold him back. He gives all for all and possesses all in all since he rests in Him who is supreme and from whom all good things proceed and flow.

[3]Ps. 119:111 [4]Ps. 59:16 [5]Matt. 11:30 [6]1 John 4:7

Love does not dwell on the gifts received but turns directly to their giver. Love knows no measure but exceeds all measure. Love feels no burden; it makes light of labor and strives to do more than it is able. Love considers nothing impossible and sees itself equal to every task.

Love, therefore, can do all things and finds itself successful where others, without love, often faint and fall prostrate.

5. Love keeps watch, and even while resting it sleeps not; it may be tired but not fatigued; it may feel under pressure, but not crushed; it may be afraid but not terrified. Like a living flame and burning torch, love always makes its way upward into the open air and blazes forth.

Whoever is in love recognizes love's voice and the most powerful appeal to God is the soul's burning love crying out to Him: "My God, my Love, *You are all mine and I am all Yours.*"[7]

6. Deepen my love so that I may learn to savor in my inmost being how sweet it is to love, how sweet it is to be dissolved and float on a sea of love. Let love take possession of me and let me rise far above myself with unheard of fervor and wonder.

Let me sing love's canticle[8] and let me follow You, my Beloved, to the very heights. Let my soul become lost in praising You and in rejoicing in Your love. Let me love You more than I love myself, and let me love myself only for the love of You. In You, let me love all who truly love You as the law of love, which radiates from You, commands me to do.

7. Love is swift, honest, devout, pleasing, and full of delight; it is strong, patient, faithful, prudent, long-suffering, manly, and never self-seeking.[9] When a man does seek himself, he forsakes love.

[7]Song 2:16 [8]Is. 5:1 [9]Cf. 1 Cor. 13:4-7

Love is cautious, humble, and upright; it is neither soft, fickle, nor given to trifling matters. It is sober, chaste, steadfast, tranquil, and keeps watch over the senses.

Love is submissive and obedient to superiors, for in its own eyes it is mean and contemptible. It is devoted and grateful to God, always trusting and hoping in Him, even when it does not taste God's sweetness. There is no being in love where there is no sorrow!

8. The person who is not prepared to suffer all things and stand fast by the will of his Beloved does not deserve to be called a lover. A lover should, for the sake of his Beloved, most willingly take on whatever is hard and bitter and never turn himself away from Him, no matter how difficult his life may be.

6. *The Proof of a True Lover*

Jesus:

Son, as yet you are neither a courageous nor a wise lover.

Disciple:

How is that Lord?

Jesus:

Because, whenever you meet even the slightest opposition you stop what you are doing and anxiously look about you for consolation. A courageous lover remains steadfast in temptation and puts no credence in the devil's warm, persuasive words. Just as I am the lover's delight in time of prosperity, I am likewise his delight in the time of adversity.

2. A wise lover considers not so much the lover's gift as the giver's love. He attends more to the giver's affection than to the gift's value, and places his beloved above all the gifts he bestows. A noble lover does not remain content with the gift, rather he desires Me whom he values above every gift.

If you sometimes feel less tenderness toward Me and My saints — less than you would like — all is not lost, for that good and sweet feeling, which you sometimes experience, is the result of My grace working in you, and is a foretaste of what you will one day enjoy in your heavenly home. But do not rely too heavily on such feelings, for they come and go.

To fight against all evil thoughts that come to mind and to reject all the devil's suggestions is a sure sign of virtue and something worthy of great merit.

3. Therefore, let no strange imaginings trouble you, no matter what kind they be, but firmly keep to your resolution and maintain your right intention toward God. It is not an illusion on your part that you are sometimes suddenly taken on high into rapture and then abruptly returned here below to again face the foolishness that usually fills your heart. You must learn to endure such thoughts rather than encourage them, and as long as you take no delight in them and resist them, they bring you merit and are not held against you.

4. Know that the ancient enemy, the devil, makes every effort to put an end to your deep desire to do good and tries to allure you from your religious devotions, such as honoring the saints, devoutly meditating on My passion, recalling your sins with spiritual profit, keeping watch over your heart, and continuing in your determination to advance in virtue.

The devil instills many evil thoughts to frighten you and to wear you out and, thus, to pull you from prayer and from reading holy and worthwhile books. He despises every humble confession of sin and, if he were able, he would like to prevent you from receiving Holy Communion.

Do not believe his words nor pay any attention to him, no matter how frequently he sets his snares to entrap you. And when he does suggest foul and wicked things to you, give it right back to him, saying: "*Get out of here, you foul-mouthed spirit,*[1] you obscene tempter! You are nothing but filth to utter such gross things into my ears. Get away from me, you vile corruptor; you shall have no part of me! *Jesus is with me, and as a valiant warrior*[2] He will reduce you to utter helplessness. I would rather die and suffer all kinds of torments than to give in to you! Be quiet and keep still! I will hear no more from you even though you continue to harass me. *The Lord is my light and my salvation; whom shall I fear.*[3] *Though an entire army encamp against me, my heart shall not be afraid.*[4] *The Lord is my helper and my redeemer.*"[5]

5. *Fight like a true soldier*[6] and if you sometimes collapse because of some frailty on your part, get right up again and with greater courage look forward to My additional grace. Take special care not to yield to useless self-satisfaction or pride, for many individuals have been led into error through pride and at times have fallen into a blindness of heart that was almost incurable. This is the ruin that awaits the proud and those who stupidly rely on themselves. Let this be a warning to you to always keep yourself humble.

[1]Matt. 4:10 [2]Jer. 20:11 [3]Ps. 27:1 [4]Ps. 27:3
[5]Ps. 19:14 [6]2 Tim. 2:3

7. *Grace and Humility*

Jesus:

Son, it is safer and more advantageous to you if you keep secret the grace of devotion, that is, do not go about putting on airs, nor speaking boastfully about it, nor esteeming it too highly. In fact, you should despise yourself the more and be somewhat wary, since it has been given to one who does not deserve it. Do not count too heavily upon such holy feelings for you may soon find yourself without them. Rather, at the time you are enjoying this grace, think how poor and miserable you were when you were without it.

Progress in the spiritual life does not consist so much in the possession of the grace of consolation as it does in the following: being able, with humility and patient resignation, to live without it, not becoming lazy with regard to your prayers, nor giving up the devotional exercises you are accustomed to perform. Continue in these exercises and prayers as seems best to you and as best you can, and never neglect your spiritual progress because of any dryness of soul or any anxiety of mind you may feel.

2. Many men become impatient and yield to sloth when things do not go according to their plans. *The road a man must walk is not always of his own choosing.*[1] It belongs to God to give comfort, when He wills, to whom He wills, and as much as He wills — all according to His good pleasure and not more.

Some individuals, because of their imprudence in relying too strongly on this grace of devotion, have brought ruin upon themselves. Not taking into account their own littleness, and

[1]Jer. 10:23

following their heart's inclinations rather than any sound judgment, they attempted to accomplish more than they were capable of.

Because they presumed to achieve more than what was pleasing to God, they quickly forfeited that grace. They thought of building nests for themselves in heaven, but have become poor and destitute, and in their shame and disgrace have learned not to attempt to soar on high with their own wings, but with confident heart to remain *nestled beneath My wings.*[2]

Those who are somewhat young and inexperienced in the way the Lord operates in souls can easily be deceived and come to ruin if they refuse to be guided by the counsel of wise men.

3. If these young men insist on following their own opinions rather than those of the more experienced, they will certainly, as long as they refuse to set aside their personal views, meet with a perilous end.

Those who think themselves wise[3] are rarely humble enough to allow others to guide them. It is better to be a blockhead and a numskull, and to be humble about it, than to possess encyclopedic knowledge and be filled with self conceit. Better to have little than much, if much is going to make you proud.

The man who devotes himself entirely to merriment by forgetting his former poverty, acts most imprudently, for he at the same time forgets that chaste fear of God that dreads the loss of graces already received. Nor is that man wise who, during difficult and grave times, yields to despair and thinks thoughts and harbors feelings that give no evidence of trust in Me.

[2]Ps. 91:4 [3]Rom. 11:25

4. The man who wants to be totally surrounded by security in peacetime is often found to be most depressed and filled with fear in time of war.

If you knew how to stay humble and small, and keep your mind under proper control, you would not so easily fall into dangerous situations.

This is the point to remember: while you experience this fervor think how you will feel when this light is taken from you. And when this happens realize that the light, which I have withdrawn for a time as a warning to you and for My glory, may again be given you.

5. Such a trial is often more helpful than if you always met with success by following your own will. An individual's true value is not measured by the number of visions or consolations he has, nor by his profound knowledge of Scripture, nor by his receiving great honors. Rather, his value is measured in this manner: Is he grounded in true humility and is he filled with divine charity? Does he always, purely and entirely, seek God's honor? Does he see himself as nothing and sincerely despise himself? Finally, does he find more joy in accepting humiliations and reproaches than in accepting honors?

8. *Having a Low Opinion of One's Self*

Disciple:

Though I am but dust and ashes, I will speak to my Lord.[1] If I esteem myself more than ashes, You are of a different opinion; in fact, my very sins are witnesses against me and I am unable to contradict their testimony. But if I belittle myself, think of

[1]Gen. 18:27

myself as nothing, throw off all self-regard and account myself to be dust, as I truly am, then Your grace will come upon me and Your light will enter my heart, and all self-esteem, no matter how infinitesimal it be, will be drowned in my total nothingness and disappear forever.

It is within my very depths that You reveal me to myself: what I am, what I have been, and what I have become. I am nothing and I never knew it! Left to myself I am but a zero and abound with frailties, but when you turn Your face toward me I suddenly gain strength and am filled with new joy. It astounds me when I realize that You are so quick to raise me up and embrace me, who am always sinking to the bottom because of the heaviness of my sins.

2. It is Your love that does this for me; it precedes me in all that I do, helps me in my many needs, guards me from grave dangers, and delivers me, as I most happily admit, from evils beyond all counting.

By loving myself, as I should not have, I lost myself; by seeking only You and by loving You with an untarnished love, I found both You and myself, and through this love I have more fully brought myself to total nothingness.

My dearest Lord, You treat me far better than I deserve and beyond all I dare hope or ask for.

My God, may You be blessed for ever! Though I am unworthy to receive anything good, nevertheless, Your liberality and infinite goodness never cease doing good, even toward the ungrateful who have turned their backs upon You. Turn us again toward You so that we may be grateful, humble, and devoted to You, *who alone are our salvation,*[2] *our power, and our strength.*[3]

[2]Is. 33:2 [3]Ps. 46:1

9. *Referring All Things to God as to Their Last End*

Jesus:

My son, if you desire to be truly blessed, then I must be your Supreme and Final End. By referring everything to Me, you cleanse your affections which much too frequently incline toward yourself and creatures. Whenever you seek yourself you will, and without any delay, begin to grow faint and wither away.

Therefore, refer all things to Me as their beginning, for it is I who have given all to you. Look upon everything as flowing from the Supreme Good, and realize that everything must return to Me as to its source.

2. All men, whether great or small, rich or poor, *draw living water from Me,*[1] as from a flowing fountain, and those who serve me freely and willingly *receive grace upon grace.*[2] But the man who seeks to glory in anything other than Me, or seeks his delight in some good of his own choosing, shall never find true joy nor have joy bursting in his heart, but shall meet obstacle after obstacle and find himself inextricably entangled in life's web.

Therefore, do not attribute anything good to yourself, nor ascribe importance to any man, but assign everything to God, without whom man has absolutely nothing. I have given you everything and I desire that everything revert back to Me; I also ask gratitude of heart in return for all that I have given you.

3. This is the truth that puts an end to all vainglory: If

[1]John 4:14 [2]John 1:16

heavenly grace and true love find a place in your heart there will be no room for envy or rancor, nor shall self-love have any claim on you. Divine love overcomes everything and deepens the powers of the soul.

If you are truly wise you will find joy in Me alone and you will put your trust only in Me. *No one is good, but only God,*[3] and He is to be praised above all things and blessed in all things.

10. *The Sweetness of Serving God*

Disciple:

I will speak once more, O Lord, and will not keep silent. I will say, in the hearing of my God, my Lord and my King, who dwells on high, *How great is the abundance of Your sweetness, O Lord, which You have laid up for those who fear You.*[1] But what are You to those who love You? To those who serve You with all their heart?

The sweetness of contemplating You, O Lord, which You give to those who love You, is beyond words to express. You showed me Your love's special sweetness in this way: You brought me into being when I was yet not, and when I wandered away from You, You brought me back that I could serve You; You also instructed me in how to love You.

2. O Fountain of eternal love, what can I say to You? How can I forget You when You continued to remember me even after I wasted away and became lost? You manifested Your mercy to Your servant beyond all expectations and granted him Your grace and friendship beyond all his deserts. *What*

[3]Luke 18:19 [1]Ps. 31:19

return shall I make to You for such a grace?[2] The grace to renounce all things and to leave the world and enter the monastic life, is not granted every individual.

Is my serving You, whom all creation is bound to serve, something special? To serve You does not appear so special to me; rather, what is outstanding and marvelous is that You have chosen one so pitiable and unworthy for Your service and have numbered him among your beloved servants.

3. *All that I have is Yours*[3] and with this I am to serve You. But the reality is quite different for You serve me rather than my serving You. Both heaven and earth, which You created for man's use, await Your word and daily they fulfill Your every command. Moreover, *You have appointed the angels to serve man*,[4] and even more amazing, You Yourself have deigned to serve man and have promised to give Yourself to him.

4. What shall I give You in return for these thousands and thousands of favors? Would that I could serve You all the days of my life! Would that I were able to serve You worthily, even for a day!

You are truly *worthy of all service, all honor, and eternal praise.*[5] You are indeed my Lord, and I am but Your poor servant who is bound to serve You with all his being and never grow weary of praising You. This is my desire and my will and whatever I lack in willpower, I ask You to supply me.

I see it as a great honor and glory to serve You and to despise all things for Your sake. Those who willingly submit themselves to Your most holy service shall receive great graces. Those who have cast aside all bodily pleasures, because of their love for You, shall enjoy the sweet consolation of the Holy

[2]Ps. 116:12 [3]1 Chr. 29:14 [4]Ps. 91:11 [5]Rev. 4:11

Spirit; and those who choose *to walk along the narrow path,*[6] and ignore all worldly affairs for Your name's sake, shall possess great freedom of soul.

5. How delightful and pleasant is this service of God that makes man truly free and holy. How holy it is to serve God as a monk for it makes a man equal to the angels, pleasing to God, terrible to the devils, and a model to other men. How desirable and lovable is that service, since it gains for us the Supreme Good and gives us a joy that endures forever.

11. Examining and Controlling the Heart's Desires

Jesus:

My son, you still have many things to learn which you have not yet fully grasped.

Disciple:

What things, Lord?

Jesus:

You must conform all your desires to My good pleasure and stop loving yourself, and earnestly desire that *My will be done.*[1]

You frequently burn with desires that powerfully impel you to action, but what is the motive behind your actions? Is it My honor or is it your own self-interest? If I be the motive, then you will be satisfied with whatever I decide for you; but if it be your own self-interest, then this is what puts the brake to your progress and slows you down.

[6]Matt. 7:14 [1]Matt. 6:10

2. Therefore, be careful not to rely too heavily on your own desires without first consulting Me. You may later on find that you are sorry and displeased with what once pleased you and what you once thought the better thing to do.

Not every desire that seems good has to be carried out, nor is every feeling contrary to your desires to be avoided. Even in good desires and endeavors it is sometimes necessary to hold yourself back; otherwise, overeagerness may result in dissipation of energies. At the same time, your lack of self-control may give offense to others and their opposition, in turn, may dishearten you and cause you to give up.

3. You sometimes have to resort to strong measures and manfully go against your sense appetites, disregarding what your flesh wants or does not want, and endeavor to subject it, though unwilling, to the spirit. *The flesh has to be chastised and held down*[2] until it learns to give obedience in all things, to be satisfied with little, happy with what is simple, and not grumble about any physical discomfort.

12. Acquiring Patience and Conquering Concupiscence

Disciple:

Lord God, I meet with much opposition in this life and I see that *I have great need of patience.*[1] No matter how I try to structure my life so that I could have peace, I still cannot *live without some sorrow*[2] and conflict.

[2] 1 Cor. 9:27

[1] Heb. 10:36 [2] Ps. 31:10

Jesus:

So it is, My son. I do not want you to look for a peace that is free of temptation or one that never meets with opposition, but I want you to have peace even while experiencing affliction and while being tried by tribulation.

2. If you answer that you are unable to bear much suffering, I will then ask, how will you be able to bear purgatory's fire? Always choose the lesser of two evils, and in order to escape future punishment strive, with patience and for the sake of God, to endure the evils of this present life.

Do you think the sufferings of worldly men are negligible or nonexistent? If you put this question to those whose lives are surrounded by the greatest of luxuries, you will find that the answer is negative. You say that these men enjoy many delights and attain all their desires and, therefore, they view their troubles as mere trifles. It may be true that they have all they desire, but how long do you think this will last?

3. The rich of this world *will vanish like smoke*[3] and their past joys will no longer be remembered. Even in life they did not enjoy their riches without some distress, some anxiety, or a touch of sadness, for the very objects that afforded them delight were the same that brought them pain and sorrow. And this is only just and proper since the pleasures they unrestrainedly desired and pursued were never capable of bringing complete enjoyment, since they carried with them the seeds of bewilderment and bitterness.

4. How short-lived, deceitful, disordered, and base are all these pleasures, and yet men are too blind and intoxicated to realize this. *Like dumb animals they hanker after*[4] some piddling

[3]Ps. 68:2 [4]Jude 10

pleasure that this corruptible life has to offer and, thus, hasten to their soul's death.

But you, My son, *do not follow after your base desires, but curb your appetites.*[5] *Delight in the Lord and He will give you your heart's desires.*[6]

5. If you truly desire to savor My delights and receive still greater consolation from Me, then despise all worldly things and renounce all vile pleasures. This will turn out to be a blessing for you and copious consolation will be yours.

The more you withdraw yourself from creaturely consolation, the greater and sweeter will be the comfort you find in Me. However, in the beginning, you shall not achieve this without going through some sorrow and fighting some battles.

Your old habits will be a drawback to you but they will be conquered by better habits,[7] and your flesh will grumble but the fervor of your determination will keep it in check. The *old serpent*[8] will tempt and entice you, but you will put him to flight by prayer, and by keeping yourself occupied in some worthwhile task you will cut off his main approach to you.

13. *Humble Obedience after the Example of Jesus Christ*

Jesus:

My son, whoever tries to withdraw himself from obedience at the same time withdraws himself from grace, and he who seeks to follow his own will loses the graces that are commonly given to all. If a man does not freely and spontaneously submit

[5]Sir. 18:30 [6]Ps. 37:4

[7]Cf. Augustine, *Confessions* VIII, 11 [8]Rev. 12:9

himself to his superior, it is a sure sign that he has not yet completely conquered his flesh since it goes on complaining and rebelling.

If you desire to gain mastery over your flesh you have to learn to give prompt obedience to your superior. The enemy outside you is more quickly overcome if your inner self is not torn apart by internal struggles. You are your soul's most troublesome and worst enemy, especially when you and your spirit are not in harmony. If you wish to have control over your flesh and blood you must acquire genuine self-contempt.

2. It is because you still love yourself more than you should that you are afraid to give yourself wholly to another's will. What's remarkable about submitting yourself to a man for the sake of God, when you are only dust and nothingness, and when I, the Almighty and Most High, who have created everything out of nothing, have humbly submitted Myself to man for your sake? I became the most meek and least of men that you might learn to conquer your pride by following the example of My humility.

Learn to obey, you who are only dust! You earthen clay, learn to be humble and place yourself at everyone's feet! Destroy your personal desires and submit yourself to all authority!

3. Direct your anger against yourself and do not allow puffed-up pride to get its hold on you. Show that you are humble and lowly by permitting everyone to walk over you and trample you underfoot *like mud in the street.*[1]

What have you to complain about, you *shallow man*?[2] You soiled sinner, what answer can you give those who criticize you, since you have ever so frequently offended God and

[1]Ps. 18:42 [2]James 2:20

many times over have deserved hell?

Because your soul was precious in My sight[3] *I turned my eye toward you and saved you.*[4] I preserved you because I wanted you to feel My love and always be grateful for My gifts. I wanted you to give yourself wholeheartedly to humility and true obedience, and patiently bear the contempt that others heap upon you.

14. Considering God's Secret Judgments and Not Becoming Proud Because of Our Good Works

Disciple:

O Lord, You thunder Your judgments overhead and all my bones shudder in fear and trembling. *My soul is strangely terrified;*[1] I stand frozen in amazement and believe that *the heavens themselves are not pure in Your sight.*[2]

If you did not spare the angels[3] *when you found wickedness among them,*[4] what is to become of me? If *stars have fallen from heaven,*[5] what can I, who am but dust, look forward to?

Men whose deeds were once thought worthy of praise have fallen to the lowest depths, and I have seen *men, who once partook of the bread of angels,*[6] *find delight in the swill fed to swine.*[7]

2. There is no holiness, O Lord, if You withdraw Your comforting hand. No wisdom is beneficial to us unless You direct it. No strength is sufficient for us unless You supply it.

[3] 1 Sam. 26:21 [4] Ezek. 20:17

[1] Job 37:1-2 [2] Job 15:15 [3] 2 Pet. 2:4 [4] Job 4:18

[5] Rev. 6:13 [6] Ps 78:25 [7] Luke 15:16

No chastity is without peril unless You protect it. No watchfulness over ourselves is advantageous to us *unless You Yourself watch over us.*[8]

When You are not with us, *we sink and perish,*[9] but when You visit us we rise up and live again. Of ourselves we are unstable, but You steady us; we are lukewarm, but You set us on fire.

3. What humble and modest opinion I ought to have of myself, and of how little worth I ought to judge the good qualities I may seem to possess. How deeply I ought to submit myself to Your *fathomless judgments*[10] to discover that I am nothing but nothingness. Yes, nothing! You, Lord, are immeasurably vast and great, and I am nothing. You are a boundless unnavigable sea wherein I discover that I am absolutely nothing.

Do I have any excuse for pride to remain concealed within me? Where now is my reliance on imagined virtue? All this useless boasting of mine is annihilated in the depths of Your judgments upon me.

4. *What is all flesh in Your sight?*[11] Shall the completed clay pot get the credit and not the potter who fashioned it?[12] Can the man whose heart is truly obedient to God ever be puffed up with empty pride? Nothing in this world will make him, whom Truth has subjected to Itself, yield to pride, nor will the man who has firmly placed his hope in God be moved by the praises of other men. The men who utter these praises are themselves nothing, and they shall pass away as the very sounds they speak, but only *the truth of the Lord endures forever.*[13]

[8]Ps. 127:1 [9]Matt. 8:25 [10]Ps. 36:6 [11]1 Cor. 1:29
[12]Cf. Is.45:9; 29:16 [13]Ps. 117:2

15. How To Pray for What We Desire

Jesus:

My son, at all times pray in this manner: "*Lord, if this pleases You, then, so let it be.*[1] If it be to Your honor, Lord, let this be done in Your name. If You, Lord, see that it will help me and think that it will profit me, then grant it so that I could use it for Your honor; but if You see that it will prove harmful to me and be of no help in saving my soul, then take this desire from me."

Not every desire, even though each may appear to men to be good and honest, proceeds from the Holy Spirit. It is rather difficult to distinguish whether a good or an evil spirit is urging you to desire this or that object, or whether you are being moved to it by your own spirit. Many who at first thought they were being led by a good spirit found in the end that they were deceived.

2. Therefore, whenever something enters your mind and seems desirable, see that you desire and ask for it with humility and with a heart filled with reverent fear of God. Give up your own will and leave everything to Me, saying: "Lord, You know what is best for me, let everything be done according to Your will. Do whatever You will, in the amount You will, and when You will. Deal with me as You best think, as best pleases You, and is most for Your glory. Put me wherever you will and treat me in all things as freely as You will. I am in Your hand; turn me around whichever way You will. *I am your servant*[2] and ready to do anything for You. I wish to live, not for myself, but for You; if only I could fittingly and perfectly serve You!"

[1]James 4:15 [2]Ps. 119:125

Disciple:

Prayer that God's Will Be Done

3. Most gentle Jesus, grant me Your grace; let it be with me, work with me, and remain with me until the end. Grant me always to desire and will what is most acceptable and most pleasing to You. Let Your will be mine, and let my will ever follow Yours and be in perfect harmony with it. Let my willing and not willing be the same as Yours and let me not be able to will or not will anything that is contrary to what You Yourself will or do not will.

4. Grant me to die to all worldly things, and for the love of You to look forward to being despised and counted as a nobody in this world. Grant me my greatest desire: to rest in You and that my heart find its peace in You.[3] You are the heart's true peace and its only rest, and apart from You everything else is cold and hard.[4] In the peace that is You, my Supreme and Everlasting Good, *I find sleep and take my rest.*[5] Amen.

16. *True Consolation Is To Be Sought in God Alone*

Disciple:

Whatever consolation I can imagine or desire I look for not in this present life but in the one to come. It is certain that if I alone had all this world's comforts and were able to enjoy all its pleasures, they would not last very long.

[3]Cf. Augustine, *Confessions* I, 1 [4]*Ibid.* VI, 16 [5]Ps. 4:8

Hence, my soul, you cannot find complete consolation nor total refreshment except in God, who consoles the poor and sustains the humble. Just wait a while longer, my soul, wait for the fulfillment of God's promise and you will enjoy an abundance of good things in heaven. If you desire the good things of this present life more than you should, you will lose those of heaven and eternity. Make use of temporal things, but desire eternal things. Temporal goods will never fully satisfy you because you were not created for their sole enjoyment.

2. Even if you possessed all created goods, this still could not make you happy and blessed for your joy and beatitude is in God, the Creator of all things. This is not the happiness that the lovers of this world praise and extol, but the happiness that Christ's good and faithful followers seek and of which the pure of heart, *whose conversation is in heaven,*[1] sometimes have a foretaste.

All human consolation is short-lived and empty; but true and blessed is that consolation that is interiorly received from Truth Itself.

The devout man carries Jesus, his consoler, with him wherever he goes, and says to him: "Lord Jesus, be with me in all places and at all times. Let my willing renunciation of all human comfort be my consolation. And if I find that I am without Your consolation, then let Your will and the trial You send me be a greater consolation to me for *You will not always chide me, nor will You keep Your anger forever.*"[2]

[1]Phil. 3:20 [2]Ps. 103:9

17. Placing All One's Cares on God

Jesus:

Son, since I know what is best for you, let Me do with you as I will. You think as a man thinks, and on many occasions you judge as human affection prompts you to judge.

Disciple:

What You say is true, Lord, and Your concern for me is much greater than any concern I could possibly have for myself, and the man who does not *place all his cares on You*[1] falters as he tries to stand on his feet.

Lord, as long as my will remains firm and steadfast toward You, do with me whatever pleases You. And whatever You choose to do can only be for my good.

2. If You desire me to abide in darkness, may You be blessed, and if You desire me to be in the light, again be blessed! If You choose to comfort me, may You be blessed, and if You wish me to suffer trials, be equally blessed, and blessed for all eternity!

Jesus:

My son, if you desire to walk with Me, remain firm in this attitude of yours. You have to be as ready and willing to suffer as you are to rejoice; you have to be as eager to be poor and in need as you are to be rich and have plenty.

Disciple:

3. Lord, I will freely suffer for You whatever You choose to send me. Because my heart is indifferent I am ready to accept

[1] 1 Pet. 5:7

from Your hand *both good and evil*,[2] sweet and bitter, joy and sorrow, and I thank You for whatever comes to me.

Keep me from all sin and I will fear neither death nor hell;[3] only *do not cast me off forever*[4] nor *blot my name from the book of life*.[5] No matter what trials befall me, none shall hurt me.

18. *Bearing This Life's Trials with Patience after the Example of Christ*

Jesus:

My son, *I came down from heaven to save you*.[1] It was out of love and not out of any need that I took your miseries upon Myself, and I did it so that you could learn patience and be able to endure life's miseries without complaint.

From the hour of My birth to that of My death on the cross I was never without some sorrow. During My life I had very little of this world's goods, and many and frequent were the complaints I heard uttered against Me. This shame and derision I endured with meekness, and in return for My kindness I was rewarded with ingratitude, for My miracles I was covered with blasphemies, and for My teaching I was reviled.

Disciple:

2. Lord, because You were patient during Your lifetime and especially in fulfilling Your Father's command, it is fitting that I, a miserable sinner, follow Your example in accepting everything with patience and bear for my salvation, and as long as it pleases You, the burdens of this corruptible life.

[2]Job 2:10 [3]Cf. Ps. 23:4 [4]Ps. 77:7 [5]Rev. 3:5
[1]John 3:17

Though this present life is felt to be a burden it has by Your grace become wonderfully meritorious, and by Your example and the paths trodden by Your saints it has become more bearable and somewhat lighter for those of us who are weak.

It likewise offers us much more consolation than it formerly did under the Old Law, when heaven's gate remained closed, when the way to heaven was enshrouded in mist, and only a few individuals were interested in seeking the kingdom of heaven. Besides, in those days even the just, who were one day to be saved, were not able to enter your heavenly kingdom until Your passion and holy death would pay the ransom price.

3. What a great debt of gratitude I owe to You for having so kindly pointed out to me and all Your faithful ones the good and the true path to Your eternal kingdom! Your life points out our way, and in holy patience we walk toward You who are our crown.

If You had not gone before us and taught us the way, who would have taken the trouble to follow it? Many, if they had not Your marvelous example before them, would have, unfortunately, remained far behind.

We have heard of *your many wonderful miracles*[2] and Your teaching, and still we are lukewarm. What would it have been like if we never had *this great light to show us the way of following You?*[3]

[2]John 12:37 [3]John 8:12

19. *Bearing Injuries Is the Proof of True Patience*

Jesus:

What are you saying, My son? Stop complaining and think of My passion and the sufferings of My saints. *So far you have not shed any of your blood in the struggle.*[1]

Your sufferings are quite small when compared to those who have endured so much, who were so vehemently tempted, so grievously afflicted, and so frequently tried and tested.

You should keep in mind the grave sufferings of others so that you could more easily bear the trifling sufferings that are yours. And if they do not appear to you to be so insignificant, then maybe it is your unwillingness to suffer them that makes them so great. But whether they be slight or serious bear them all with patience.

2. The better you ready yourself for suffering, the more wisely you act and the more merit you gain. Once your mind is sufficiently disposed toward suffering, you will bear it more easily. And do not say: "I cannot bear such an action coming from such a man, nor do I have to put up with it. He has seriously wounded me, charging me with things I never would have dreamed. But if it came from another individual, I could take it in stride and say that it was just something that had to be endured in life."

Such thinking is foolish because it disregards both the virtue of patience as well as Him from whom that patience is to receive its crown. Likewise it morbidly dwells on the injury and on the one who inflicted it.

[1]Heb. 12:4

3. The man who is only willing to suffer what seems good to him and only from individuals of his own choosing is not a truly patient man. The true man of patience does not care who the individual is who tries him, whether he be his superior, equal, or one of lesser state, or whether he be a good and holy man or one who is wicked and perverse. No matter how much or how often adversity befalls him through the creatures of this world, he accepts them all with equal joy as coming from the hand of God and considers it to be to his advantage, for nothing suffered for God's sake — no matter how small it be — goes without its reward.

4. Therefore, if you want to enjoy the victory, be ready for the fighting. *You cannot win your crown of patience without some struggle.*[2] If you refuse suffering, you also refuse the crown; but if you desire the crown, then fight like a man and do it with patience. Where there is no labor, there is no rest! Where there is no fighting, there is no victory!

Disciple:

5. O Lord, make it possible for me to accomplish with Your grace what is impossible for me by nature.[3] You know the little I can bear and when some small trial comes my way I immediately fall apart. Make the bearing of trials something desirable and lovable to me, for suffering and affliction for Your name is wholesome to my soul.

[2] 2 Tim. 2:5 [3] Cf. Luke 18:27

20. *Acknowledging Our Weakness and the Miseries of This Life*

Disciple:

Lord, I will confess my weakness to You, *I will acknowledge my sinfulness.*[1] Often it is only a small thing that troubles and depresses me, and in my heart I determine to act more courageously in the future; but when a slight temptation does come my way, I find myself filled with apprehension. Simple matters can at times give rise to serious temptations, and when I think that I am somewhat safe because I am not then under fire, I soon find myself almost blown over by a gentle breeze.

2. Therefore, Lord, look upon my weakness and wretchedness, for both are indeed well known to You. Have pity on me and *pull me out of this mire before I become imbedded in it*[2] and totally dejected. The fact that I am so unstable and am but a weakling — when it comes to resisting my passions — embarrasses and shames me in Your sight.

Though I do not altogether consent to these temptations, nevertheless, their pursuit after me is most annoying and so distressing that I grow weary living under such constant tension. I fully recognize that I am weak for fierce imaginings stampede into my mind with greater speed than they show in leaving it.

3. Most powerful God of Israel, ardent Lover of all faithful souls, look upon the labors and sorrows of Your servant and assist him in all his undertakings.

Strengthen me with courage from heaven, lest the old man — that miserable flesh of mine — not yet fully subjected to

[1] Ps 32:5 [2] Ps 69:14

the spirit and against which I must fight with my every breath, rise up and get the upper hand.

What kind of a life is this, where miseries and afflictions are never lacking, and where everything is a snare or an enemy? When one trial or temptation passes, another comes, and even while the first is still in the process of attack, many others unexpectedly join in to besiege us.

4. How is it possible to love such a life, filled with so much sadness and subject to so many miseries and misfortunes? How can we even give it the name of life since it brings with it so many plagues and deaths? Yet many people love this life and seek their full delight in it. They may frequently charge the world with being artificial and empty, but these same people are not eager to leave it. Why? Because the desires of the flesh have complete dominion over them.

There are some things that draw men to love the world and there are others that lead them to despise it. *The lust of the flesh, the concupiscence of the eyes, and the pride of life*[3] all draw men to love the world, but the pains and miseries that rightly flow from these desires engender a weariness of and a hatred for it.

5. Unfortunately, sinful pleasures have so complete a control over the worldly man that he thinks it an utter delight to be caught among such prickly briars. He is of this opinion, however, only because he has never tasted the sweetness of God nor has he ever experienced the inner beauty of virtue.

But those who perfectly despise the world and strive to live for God under the discipline of a superior, experience the divine sweetness promised those who have renounced all things, and who see most clearly how terribly mistaken the world is and in how many ways it is being deceived.

[3] 1 John 2:16

21. *We Must Rest in God Above All Other Good Gifts*

Disciple:

My soul, in and above all things find your rest in God, for He is the saints' eternal rest.

Prayer

Most sweet and loving Jesus, grant me to rest in You above every other creature; above all health and beauty, above all honor and glory, above all power and dignity, above all science and wisdom, above all wealth and talent, above all joy and gladness, above all fame and praise, above all sweetness and consolation, above all hope and promise, above all merit and desire, above all the gifts and favors You offer and shower upon me, above all the happiness and joy the mind can perceive and understand, and finally, above angels and archangels, above the entire host of heaven, above all things visible and invisible. Above everything that is not You, my God.

2. O Lord, my God, You are over and above all things. You alone are most high; You alone are most powerful; You alone are totally self-sufficient and complete; You alone are most sweet and full of consolation.

You alone are most beautiful and most lovable; You alone are most noble and above everything else most glorious. In You all good things exist and perfectly exist; they always have and always will.

Whatever You give me other than Yourself, or whatever You reveal to me or promise me, is much too little and is insufficient for me unless I see You and fully possess You. My heart, for certain, cannot find its true rest nor be perfectly happy unless it rises above all gifts and all creatures and rests in You.[1]

3. My most sweet Spouse, Jesus Christ, most pure Lover, Lord of all creation, *who will give me the wings of true freedom to fly toward You and find my rest in You?*[2]

When will I be fully free *to see how sweet You are, my Lord God?*[3]

When will I become so fully absorbed in You that, for the love of You, I will no longer be conscious of myself but only of You, and in a way that surpasses the powers of my senses and is not granted all men to experience?

I often complain and bear my uneasiness with a sad heart. Countless evils befall me in this vale of tears, and very often they disturb me, depress me, and darken my way. They distract me and slow me down, entice me and so entangle me that I am no longer free to go to You, nor anymore do I enjoy the sweet embraces You are accustomed to grant the souls of the blessed.

Let the cry of my heart and the many desolations I suffer on earth find a favorable hearing with You!

4. O Jesus, splendor of eternal glory and comfort of the pilgrim soul, I am voiceless before You, but I will have my silence speak to You.

How long will my Lord delay in coming? May He come to me, His most needy servant, and gladden my heart. May He stretch forth His hand and deliver me, unfortunate as I am, from all distress.

Come to me, come! Without You, no hour or day is joyous! You are my joy and without You I have no one to share my table.

[1]Cf. Augustine, *Confessions* I, 1 [2]Ps. 55:6 [3]Ps. 34:8

Misery is mine; I feel I am a prisoner fettered down with heavy chains. I wait for the light of Your presence to refresh me; turn Your kind face toward me and set me free.

5. Let others seek things other than You, as it pleases them, but nothing delights me nor will anything ever delight me, except You, my God, my hope and eternal salvation. I will not remain silent, nor will I cease offering my prayers until You again send me Your grace and inwardly speak to me.

Jesus:

I am here, My son. I have come because you have invited Me. Your tears and the yearnings of your soul, together with your humility and contrite heart, have all moved Me and brought Me to you.

Disciple:

Lord, I called You because I desired to delight in You; I am now prepared to renounce all things for You.

You first inspired me to seek You. Therefore, Lord, may You be blessed for having shown Your goodness to Your servant *according to the multitude of Your mercies.*[4]

6. What more does Your servant have to say in Your presence, except that he wishes to humble himself profoundly before You, always aware of his wickedness and wretchedness.

Amid all the wonders of heaven and earth, *there is no one like You.*[5] Your works are exceedingly good, *Your judgments are true,*[6] and by Your providence You rule the universe.

Therefore, praise and glory to You, who are the Wisdom of the Father; may my lips, my soul, and everything created join in praising and blessing You.

[4]Ps. 106:45 [5]Ps. 40:5 [6]Ps. 19:9

22. *Remembering God's Many Benefits to Us*

Disciple:

Lord, open my heart to Your law[1] and *teach me to walk according to Your precepts.*[2]

Grant me *to understand Your will*[3] and to remember with great reverence and due regard Your benefits, both those granted to all men and those especially given me, so that I may worthily offer You my thanks.

I well know and acknowledge that I am unable to offer You the praise and gratitude I ought, even for the least of Your benefits, for *I am much less than any of the benefits You have bestowed on me,*[4] and when I reflect upon Your excellence and Your greatness, my spirit wilts in its inadequacy.

2. Whatever we have in body and in soul and whatever inward or outward, natural or supernatural qualities we possess, all are Your benefits. Each and every one of them proclaims that You, from whom we have received everything, are generous, good, and loving.

Though some men have received more benefits and others less, still, they are all Yours, and without You we cannot have even the smallest of them. He who has received more *is not to glory as if he deserved them,*[5] nor is he to set himself over others, nor look down upon those receiving less.

The man who attributes less to himself and shows more humility and piety in returning thanks where it is due, is the greater and better man. And the man who considers himself the lowest of all, and judges himself least worthy of all, is the one who is most qualified to receive greater blessings.

[1] 2 Macc. 1:4 [2] Ezek. 20:19 [3] Eph. 5:17
[4] Gen. 32:10 [5] 1 Cor. 4:7

3. He who has received less ought not to become dejected, nor become angry, nor envious of the one who has received more. Rather, he should look to You and praise Your great goodness since You have bestowed Your gifts so freely, so willingly, so lavishly, and *without respect of persons.*[6]

All good things come from You and, therefore, You are to be praised in all things.

You know what is best for each of us, and the reason You grant more to one and less to another is not for us to comprehend; this is for You to decide since You alone know each one's merits.

4. Therefore, O God, I consider it a great blessing not to have many of those goods that in men's eyes and in outward appearance call for praise and honor. Whoever is convinced of his poverty and lowliness will not only not succumb to despondency, dejection, or depression, but will view this as a source of great joy and consolation since *You, O God, have chosen the poor,*[7] the humble, and those whom the world despises, to be Your friends and members of Your household.

The apostles whom *You have made princes over all the earth*[8] are themselves witnesses of this fact. They lived in this world, humbly and simply, without complaint, *showing neither malice nor deceit.*[9] They even *rejoiced when they suffered insults for Your name,*[10] and gladly and most lovingly did they embrace all that the world detests.

5. Nothing, therefore, ought to be a greater source of joy to him who loves You and acknowledges Your benefits, than that Your will and the good pleasure of Your eternal purposes be fulfilled in him. He is as content and happy in being accounted

[6]Rom. 2:11 [7]James 2:5 [8]Ps. 45:16 [9]1 Pet. 2:1
[10]Acts 5:41

the least of all as another is happy in being reckoned the greatest.

He is as fully satisfied and at peace when he is in the last place as when he is in the first;[11] as glad when he is despised and rejected, devoid of name and reputation, as another is elated when accounted great and honorable in the world. Your will and the love of Your honor take precedence over everything else and are a great consolation and more agreeable to him than all the benefits You have up to now granted him and will grant in the future.

23. *Four Things That Bring Great Peace*

Jesus:

My son, I will now teach you the way of peace and true liberty.

Disciple:

Lord, do as You say, for this is what I most eagerly want to hear.

Jesus:

Always strive, My son, to do another's will rather than your own.[1]

Always choose to have less rather than more.[2]

Always seek the lowest place[3] and be submissive in all things.

Always desire and pray that God's will be entirely fulfilled in you.[4]

[11]Cf. Luke 14:10 [1]Cf. Matt. 26:39 [2]Cf. Matt. 10:10
[3]Cf. Luke 14:10 [4]Cf. Matt. 6:10

The man who accomplishes all this advances toward peace and rest.

Disciple:

2. Lord, this discourse of Yours, though brief, has the soul of perfection in it. It may have few words but it is full of meaning and rich with fruitfulness.

If I could faithfully follow Your words, I would not be so easily upset. Whenever I feel uneasy and sluggish I find that it is because I have strayed from Your teaching.

But You, O Lord, *who can accomplish all things*[5] and always love to see the soul make spiritual progress, grant me a still greater grace, namely, that I may be able to fulfill Your instructions and thus achieve salvation.

A Prayer against Evil Thoughts

3. *My Lord and God, be not far from me; my God, hasten to help me,*[6] for *a throng of thoughts have risen up against me*[7] and great fears plague my soul. How shall I ever pass through them unhurt? How shall I ever break their power over me?

Jesus:

I will go before you and will humble the great ones of the earth.[8] I will open prison doors for you and to you I will reveal hidden secrets.

Disciple:

Lord, do as You say, and let all evil thoughts flee before Your face. My fond hope and only consolation is to make You

[5]Job 42:2 [6]Ps. 71:12 [7]Ps. 27:12 [8]Is. 45:2-3

my refuge in every affliction, to confide in You, to call upon You from the depths of my heart, and patiently await Your comforting gift.

A Prayer for the Mind's Enlightenment

4. O good Jesus, shine on me with the brightness of Your internal light and expel all darkness from the mansions of my heart. Restrain my many wandering thoughts and destroy the temptations that assail me.

Use Your strength in fighting for me, and suppress those wicked beasts — those seductive sensual desires of mine. Establish peace in me and let fulsome praise of You resound throughout those sacred precincts found in a clear conscience.

Command the winds and tempests to obey. To the sea say "*Be still!*" and to Aquilo, the north wind, "*Stop gusting!*" *and there will be a great calm.*[9]

5. *Send forth Your light and truth*[10] to shine on the earth, but until You enlighten me, I am as the earth *empty and void.*[11]

Send down Your grace from above and water my heart with heaven's dew; pour down the waters of devotion to steep the face of the earth and may it bring forth good and perfect fruit.

Raise up my mind, loaded down with the heavy weight of sin, and lift my thoughts to heavenly things. Once I have tasted the sweetness of celestial happiness, I am ashamed to think of terrestrial things.

6. Draw me and deliver me from all fleeting creaturely comforts, for no created object can fully satisfy me nor console me.

[9]Mark 4:39 [10]Ps. 43:3 [11]Gen. 1:2

Unite me to You by an inseparable bond of love. You alone can satisfy the lover and without You all things are utterly worthless.

24. *Avoiding Curiosity about Other People's Lives*

Jesus:

My son, do not give in to curiosity nor waste your time on useless things. What does this or that affair have to do with you? Your duty is *to follow Me.*[1]

Why concern yourself whether a certain individual is such and such a man, or whether another speaks or acts in this or that way? You are not required to answer for another's actions but are required *to give an account of your own,*[2] so why meddle in other people's business?

I know every living individual and *I see all that happens under the sun;*[3] I know how each man fares, how he thinks, what he desires, and what his intentions are.[4] Therefore, leave everything to Me. As for yourself, keep yourself in quiet peace. Let the nosey busybody scurry about as much as he likes for he will receive a fitting recompense for all that he says and does. There is no man who can deceive Me.

2. Don't be overeager to associate with men of influence, nor to have a multitude of acquaintances, nor to enjoy the close companionship of choice friends. Such meetings engender distractions and diminish the light within you.

If you assiduously await My coming and *open the door of your*

[1]John 21:22 [2]Rom. 14:12 [3]Eccles. 1:14 [4]Cf. John 2:25

heart to Me,[5] I will gladly converse with you and reveal My mysteries to you.

Be prudent in all your dealings, watchful during prayer, and always humble!

25. *Where Certain Peace and True Progress Are To Be Found*

Jesus:

My son, I have said: *Peace I leave you; My peace I give you, not as the world gives do I give to you.*[1]

Everyone desires peace but not everyone cares about the things that belong to true peace. I give My peace to those *who are humble and meek of heart,*[2] and you can attain that peace by exercising great patience. If you hear My voice and follow it, great peace will be yours.

Disciple:

What must I then do?

Jesus:

Always attend to your own business and watch what you say and do. Direct your every effort to this end, namely, to seek only to please Me and desire nothing other than Me. Judge not rashly the words and deeds of others nor meddle in what does not pertain to you. The result will be that you will only rarely or infrequently suffer anxiety.

2. This present life is not meant to be free of all disquiet, nor

[5]Rev. 3:20

[1]John 14:27 [2]Matt. 11:29

are we never to suffer some annoyance of body or soul — such only is the state of eternal rest.

Don't think that you have arrived at true peace just because you feel no trouble weighing you down, nor judge that all is well since you are unaware of anyone working against you. And don't imagine that all is perfect just because everything seems to be going your way.

Don't put on airs, nor think you are especially beloved of God because you enjoy great devotion and interior sweetness; such gifts do not make a man a true lover of virtue, and you should know that perfection and progress in the spiritual life do not depend upon them.

Disciple:

3. On what then do they depend, Lord?

Jesus:

Spiritual progress and perfection consist in offering yourself, with your whole heart, to the divine will, and not seeking yourself in anything either small or great, in time or in eternity. Weigh everything in the same balance, and with equal serenity of heart offer thanksgiving to God in times of trial and in periods of prosperity.

Because your hope is strong and steadfast you can, when consolation will be withdrawn, prepare yourself to endure even greater trials, and don't think that you ought not to suffer so great or so many afflictions, but acknowledge that all My decisions are just and give praise to My holy name. It is only then that you will walk in the right and true path of peace and with unshakable hope look forward once again to joyfully seeing My face.[3]

[3]Cf. Job 33:26

And when you achieve a complete contempt of self know that *your peace will abound*[4] as much as is possible in this earthly life.

26. The Excellence of a Free Mind That Comes More from Humble Prayer than from Much Reading

Disciple:

Lord, the duty of the man who desires to be perfect is to keep his mind ever directed on celestial things and to walk through this world's many cares as if he had none. And he accomplishes this, not like some benumbed individual unaware of his surroundings, but as one endowed with great freedom of mind and one liberated from all unregulated love of creatures.

2. My most gracious Lord, I implore You, keep me free of the concerns of this life, otherwise, I may find myself entangled in them; deliver me from the many needs of the body so that pleasure may not ensnare me, and save me from all obstacles to my soul's progress lest I break under the strain and utterly collapse.

I am not asking to be delivered from those things that worldly individuals fanatically but foolishly pursue, but ask to be liberated from those trials which are the consequence of that common curse placed on human nature and which weigh so heavily on Your servant's soul and keep him from enjoying, as often as he would like, true freedom of mind.

[4]Ps. 72:7

3. O my God, who are unspeakable sweetness, turn to bitterness every sensual delight that takes me away from the love of eternal things and wrongly entices me to itself under the guise of being something good and desirable.

My God, let me not be overcome! Let not *flesh and blood*[1] vanquish me! Let not the world deceive me with its promise of a short-lived glory, and let not the devil's wiles play their tricks on me! Give me the strength to resist, the patience to endure, and the steadfastness to persevere.

Rather than this world's consolation give me the sweet unction of your Spirit, and instead of sensual love fill me with love for Your name.

4. Whatever the human body needs, whether it be food, drink, clothing, or other things necessary and useful for its sustenance, is all burdensome to one whose spirit burns for God.[2] But since our bodies must be sustained in life it is not permitted us to totally disregard them. At the same time, however, the holy law forbids us to ask for more than we need and to seek what is merely pleasurable. If this latter were the case, the body would then be in revolt against the spirit.

In all this, Lord, I ask You to lead me by Your hand and teach me never to yield to excess.

27. *Self-Love Keeps Us from Attaining Our Supreme Good*

Jesus:

My son, you must give all for all and keep nothing back for yourself. Realize that there is nothing more harmful to you in

[1]Gal. 1:16 [2]Cf. Bernard's *First Sermon for Septuagesima*

this world than self-love.

To the degree that you love a creature and are attached to it, to that degree it holds you back. However, if your love be pure, simple, and properly ordered, then nothing can ever hold you captive. Neither desire what you should not have, nor possess anything that could hinder you or rob you of your interior freedom.

It surprises Me that you will not, from the depths of your heart, commit yourself to Me together with all that you can possess or desire!

2. Why do you afflict yourself with useless sorrows? Why *wear yourself out*[1] with worthless worries? Remain in My good pleasure and nothing will ever harm you.

If you seek one or another object or desire to be in one or another place — all for the sake of your comfort and self-interest — know that you will never find rest, nor will you ever be free of anxious cares. Why? Because every thing carries some defect within it, and everywhere there is someone to contradict you.

3. It is not the acquiring of possessions nor their increase that helps your spiritual progress, but it is your contempt for them and your desire to cut them out of your heart that bring advancement. I refer not only to money and other wealth but also to the hunger for honors and the appetite for idle praise. All these *pass away with the world.*[2]

The very place where you are stationed helps you little if you are without spiritual fervor. And if your heart be not rooted in its true foundation, that is, in Me, the peace it has sought from the outside will not last very long. You may be able to change your place of residence but that change will not

[1]Ex. 18:18 [2]1 John 2:17

make you better. If the chance to move should present itself and you decide to take it, know that you will again face the very same thing you are now trying to avoid and, perhaps, even more.

Disciple:

Prayer for a Pure Heart and for Heavenly Wisdom

4. Uphold me, Lord, with the grace of Your Holy Spirit.[3] Give strength to my inner self[4] and empty my heart of all useless cares and concerns. Let me not be drawn by contrary desires —whether they be for something worthless or worthwhile — but let me view everything as transitory and myself passing along as well.

There is nothing lasting under the sun, but all is vanity[5] and troublesome to the spirit. How wise is the man who ponders such thoughts!

5. Lord, *give me heavenly wisdom,*[6] that I may learn to seek You in all things and find You, to relish You in all things and love You, and to understand all things as they are and as You in Your wisdom have ordained them.

Give me the prudence necessary to avoid all flatterers and the patience needed to bear with those who oppose me.

It is a sign of great wisdom *not to be tossed back and forth by men's windy words,*[7] and not to give ear to the deceptive and seductive voice of the Siren, but confidently to continue along the path we have entered upon.

[3]Cf. Ps. 51:12 [4]Cf. Eph. 3:16 [5]Eccles. 2:11
[6]Wis. 9:4 [7]Eph. 4:14

28. *Against Slanderous Tongues*

Jesus:

Don't be overly disturbed, My son, if some think poorly of you and say things that you would prefer not to hear. You ought to hold a worse opinion of yourself and believe there is none weaker than yourself.

If you are intent on following the ways of the interior life you will not give much credence to such flitting words. It requires much prudence on your part to keep silent when evil is being heaped upon you; turn inwardly to Me and do not be affected by human judgments.

2. Don't have your peace depend on what other men might say about you; whether they interpret your actions rightly or wrongly, you are still what you are.

Where will you find true peace and true glory, if not in Me?[1] The man who is neither eager to please men nor afraid to displease them is the one who will enjoy great peace.

It is in disordered loves and empty fears that all disquiet of heart and distraction of mind have their origin.

29. *In Time of Trial Call Upon God and Bless His Name*

Disciple:

Blessed be Your name, O Lord, for ever and ever! You chose this trial and temptation to come upon me, and since I am unable to escape it I must have recourse to You and ask Your help in turning it to my benefit.

[1]Cf. John 16:33

Lord, I am being assailed by tribulation; my heart is greatly distraught and my present suffering and affliction overwhelm me. Beloved Father, what now am I to say? These troubles press on me from all sides; *save me from this hour.*[1]

It is for the purpose of glorifying You that I have come to this hour,[2] an hour of deep humiliation so that I can be delivered by You. *Be pleased, O Lord, to deliver me*[3] for I am but a poor wretch. Of myself what can I do? And without You where can I go?

Give me patience, Lord, especially at this time. *Help me, O God,*[4] and I shall be without fear no matter how severely I am hard-pressed.

2. Amid these trials what am I to say, Lord? *May Your will be done!*[5] I have certainly deserved this affliction and this distress, and rightly ought I to bear them, and with patience too, until this storm passes and the good weather returns.

Your mighty hand is all powerful,[6] Lord. I know You can remove this temptation from me or decrease its force lest I die under it, just as You, my God and my Mercy, have done for me on many another occasion.

The more difficult it is for me to extricate myself from these trials, the easier it is for *the Most High's right hand to effect this change.*[7]

[1]John 12:27 [2]*Ibid.* [3]Ps. 40:13 [4]Ps. 109:26
[5]Matt. 26:42 [6]Wis. 11:17 [7]Ps. 77:10

30. *Asking God's Help and Being Confident of Regaining His Grace*

Jesus:

My son, I am the Lord, *your stronghold in the day of tribulation.*[1] Come to Me whenever things do not go well with you.[2]

The main obstacle that keeps you from receiving heaven's consolation is the fact that you are too slow in turning to prayer. Before you have decided to come to Me you have already sought consolation and comfort from outward things. And only after you have learned that creatures are of no help to you do you remember that I am the deliverer of all who hope in Me. Apart from Me there is no worthwhile help, no useful counsel, no lasting remedy.

Now that the storm is over and you have caught your breath, regain your strength in light of My mercies. I am near you, I the Lord, to restore everything to you, and not only what you previously had but to give you an overflowing abundance.

2. *Can there be anything too difficult for Me?*[3] Will I be like the *one who makes a promise and then fails to fulfill it?*[4] Where is your faith? Stand firm and persevere in your decision. Be a man of patient courage and consolation will be yours in due time. *Wait patiently for me.*[5] Yes, wait, and *I will come and heal you.*[6]

It is temptation that distresses you and unreasonable fear that frightens you. Why worry about uncertain future happenings? These only pile sorrow upon sorrow. *Sufficient for the day is the evil in it.*[7] It is useless and senseless to rejoice in, or

[1]Nahum 1:7 [2]Cf. Matt. 11:28 [3]Jer. 32:27
[4]Num. 23:19 [5]Ps. 40:1 [6]Matt. 8:7 [7]Matt. 6:34

become distressed about, some doubtful future event; it is most likely that it will never happen.

3. It may be part of being human to be taken in by such delusions, but it also clearly indicates that the soul is weak if it be so easily drawn by the devil's least suggestion. The devil cares not whether he deceives and dupes you by speaking the truth or by telling lies, or whether he conquers you by your love of something present or by your fear of something in the future. *Do not let your heart be troubled and do not be afraid.*[8]

Believe in Me,[9] and trust in My mercy. When you think you are the farthest from Me, it is then that I am nearest to you. When you think that all is lost, it is then that your victory is close at hand.

All is not lost when the result is not as you planned. Don't let your present feelings affect your judgment, and don't react to a difficulty — no matter what its source — as if there were no hope of being freed from it.

4. Don't think that you are totally abandoned if for a time I have sent you some trial or have withdrawn the consolation you sought, for this is the road that leads you to the kingdom of heaven. Doubtless, it is better for you, and for my other servants too, to undergo these trials than to have everything come out just as you desired.

I know your secret thoughts[10] and I know it is more helpful to your salvation that you sometimes be left without any interior relish, otherwise, you might begin to boast about your success, yield to self-conceit, and then think yourself better than you really are.

What I have given you I can take away, and when it pleases Me I can again restore it to you.

[8]John 14:27 [9]John 14:1 [10]Ps. 44:21

5. Though I have granted you a grace it still remains Mine, and when I withdraw it I am not taking something that belongs to you. *Every good endowment and every perfect gift is Mine.*[11]

If I send you affliction or adversity, neither complain nor become depressed for I can quickly lift up your spirits and change every burden into a joy. In all this I am just, and when I deal with you in such a manner you should still praise me.

6. If you see reality as it actually is and judge it correctly, you ought never to be dejected and troubled at adversity but ought to rejoice and give thanks. You should consider it a special joy that in sending you these sorrows I do not spare you.

I have told My beloved disciples: *as the Father has loved Me, so I love you.*[12] When I sent them out, I sent them not in search of temporal joys but to fight mighty struggles; not to look for honors but to be happy in being victims of contempt; not to seek leisure but to spend their time in laboring for others; not to desire rest but to *bear fruit with patience.*[13]

My son, take these words of Mine to heart!

31. *Setting All Creatures Aside To Find the Creator*

Disciple:

Lord, if I am to arrive at that point in the spiritual life where neither man nor creature is to be an obstacle in my way, then I need a still greater grace. As long as there is anything that holds me down I cannot freely fly to You.

[11]James 1:17 [12]John 15:9 [13]Luke 8:15

He wished to fly freely who said: *Who will give me the wings of a dove? I would fly away and be at rest.*[1] What man enjoys greater rest than the one whose sight is always directed on God? Who has greater freedom than the man who desires nothing on earth?

When a man's mind is totally taken up with God he rises above creatures, completely forgets himself, and acknowledges that among creatures there is no equal to You, his Creator.

Unless a man is set loose from all creatures he cannot freely turn himself to divine things, and the reason why there are so few who devote themselves to the contemplative life is because only a few know how to separate themselves completely from creatures and transitory things.

2. Much grace is needed to lift up the soul and carry it far above itself. Unless a man be raised in spirit, liberated from creatures, and totally united to God, then all that he knows and possesses profits him nothing.

He who esteems anything to be great, other than the One who is eternally and immeasurably good, will always remain but a paltry individual tied down to this earth of ours. Whatever is not God is nothing[2] and ought to be recognized as nothing.

There is a vast difference between the wisdom of one who is devout and divinely illumined and the knowledge of an educated and learned scholar. The knowledge that flows from above under divine influence is nobler by far than that gained through human study and research.

3. Many individuals desire to be contemplatives but they are unwilling to take the necessary steps to attain it. Their

[1]Ps. 55:6 [2]Cf. Augustine, *Confessions* XIII, 8

greatest obstacle is that they remain on the level of sign and sensible reality and give little attention to self-mortification.

I do not know by what spirit we, who claim to be spiritual men, are being led or what our goals are, when we exert so much effort and expend so much time on transitory and useless things and rarely give any thought to recollection and the interior life.

4. Sad to say, immediately after a brief period of prayerful recollection we rush from our rooms to attend to some outward activity, never thinking of submitting these external actions of ours to the strictest of scrutiny.

We pay no attention to where our affections lie nor are we saddened by the foulness of our actions. It was because *all flesh had corrupted its way*[3] that the great flood came.

Since our inner inclinations are severely corrupted, it follows that every act flowing from them is also corrupt inasmuch as it comes from a weak and defective source. But from a pure heart there flows the fruit of a good life.[4]

5. We inquire about how much a man might have accomplished in life but we never seek the motives that led him to act. We ask whether he is strong, rich, handsome, competent, or whether he is a good writer, a pleasing singer, or an energetic worker, but we refrain from asking whether he is poor in spirit, meek and patient, or how devout he is.

Nature looks at man's outward appearance but grace views his inward reality; nature is, thus, frequently misguided but grace, since it trusts in God, is never deceived.

[3]Gen. 6:12 [4]Cf. 1 Tim. 1:5

32. *Self-Denial and the Renunciation of All Desire*

Jesus:

Full liberty will never be yours, My son, *unless you totally deny yourself.*[1]

Everyone who seeks and loves only himself is held fast by heavy chains; he is a selfish busybody who always *seeks his own interests and not those of Jesus Christ.*[2] Whatever he plans or accomplishes will not last long for everything that does not come from God will certainly perish.

Hold on to this pithy but pregnant phrase: Forsake everything and you will find everything. Set all your desires aside and you will find rest. Reflect long on this point and when you have put it into practice you will understand all things.

Disciple:

2. Lord, achieving perfection is not the work of a single day nor is it child's play. That brief statement of Yours describes the goal to which every religious individual must tend.

Jesus:

My son, when you hear the way of perfection being described, do not turn away from it nor lose heart. Rather, it should impel you to seek a higher way of life or, at least, to burn with a desire for it.

I wish it were so with you, and I wish you had reached that level of perfection where you no longer loved yourself but stood ready to do My will and that of him whom I have appointed to be your father over you. You would then give Me great pleasure and would spend your life in peace and joy.

[1]Matt. 16:24 [2]Phil. 2:21

There are still many things that you must forsake, and unless you unreservedly give them up for Me, you will not receive what you ask of Me.

I urge you to buy from Me gold refined by fire that you may be rich,[3] that is, rich with the heavenly wisdom that spurns all earthly things. Set aside this earth's wisdom and the desire to please others and yourself.

3. I have instructed you to purchase for yourself what is worthless in the eyes of the world rather than what it highly esteems. Indeed, true heavenly wisdom carries little value for the man of today and, in fact, it is all but totally forgotten for it does not hold one's self in esteem nor does it seek men's praise. Though there are many who praise this wisdom with their lips, nevertheless, their manner of life in no way corresponds to their words. Heavenly wisdom is the *pearl of great price*[4] hidden from the eyes of the multitude.

33. *Our Heart's Fickleness and the Focusing of Our Attention on God*

Jesus:

My son, do not rely on your present feelings for they will soon change into something different.

As long as you live, you will always be subject to change even though you wish it were not so. Sometimes you will be happy and at other times sad; sometimes you will be at peace and at other times greatly agitated. Now you will be filled with devotion, later on you will be without all devotion; now industrious, later sluggish; now solemn, later lighthearted.

[3]Rev. 3:18 [4]Matt. 13:46

But the man who is wise and well instructed in the spiritual life stands high above these vicissitudes and gives little heed to what he himself feels or whence blows the fickle wind. Instead, he focuses his full attention on attaining his due and desired end.

2. It is possible for one and the same individual to remain in a period of protracted peace as he passes through a series of varying events. He can do this only because he has focused his attention entirely on Me. The more finely you focus your attention on Me, the greater your steadiness in passing through life's successive storms.

In many cases, however, this focus becomes blurred since the mind much too quickly becomes distracted by anything delightful that may come within its purview. Rarely will you find anyone who is altogether free of self-seeking, that natural blemish with which you were all born.

Thus it was that several Jews came to Bethany to the house of Martha and Mary *not only because of Jesus, but also to see Lazarus.*[1] Your focus, therefore, must be exact and on target, directed on Me and not on anything else that might chance to enter the range of your vision.

34. *God Is the Lover's Only Delight*

Disciple:

My God and my all![1] What more is there that I can want? What greater happiness can I desire? O words, you are sweet

[1]John 12:9

[1]These are the opening words of a prayer that may well have been written or recited by St. Francis of Assisi (1182-1226). In any case, they have become the "motto" of St. Francis and his orders.

and delightful to the one who loves the Word and *not the world nor the things of the world.*[2]

My God and my all! To him who understands, these words are sufficient; to him who loves, these words are a joy to be repeated over and over again.

Indeed, Lord, when You are present everything is a joy, and when You are absent everything is tiresome. You calm the heart; You give it great peace and fill it with festive gladness.

You make us think well of all things and make us use all things to praise You. Without You, nothing can long please us; but if something does happen to please us and is according to our taste, then Your grace must be within it and You must have seasoned it with the spice of Your wisdom.

2. To the man who takes his delight in You, what will not taste right to him? And to him who does not take delight in You, what can ever bring him joy?

Those who are wise in the ways of the world and seek their pleasure in the senses enjoy none of Your wisdom. The way of the world is absolute foolishness and *the way of the senses is death.*[3]

But those who follow You, despising the world and subduing their flesh, are the only ones who are acknowledged as truly wise; this is because they have set foolishness aside for truth and have rejected the flesh for the spirit. These individuals find their delight in God and whatever good they find in creatures they refer it back to their Creator with hearts full of praise.

Great is the difference, in fact, vast is the difference between the sweetness found in the Creator and that found in creatures. Eternity is altogether different from time, and uncreated light is totally unlike created light.

[2]1 John 2:15 [3]Rom. 8:6

Prayer

3. O Light eternal, who transcend all created light, send forth a flash of Your lightning from on high and let it penetrate my heart's inmost depths. Cleanse my spirit and give it joy, enlighten it and so vivify it that it may, with all its powers, cling to You in joyful rapture.

When will that blessed and most desired of hours come when You will fully satisfy me with Your presence, and *be all in all to me*?[4] As long as this is not granted me, my joy will not be full.

Alas, the old man still lives in me; he is neither wholly crucified[5] nor is he entirely dead. *He still battles strongly against the spirit*,[6] wages war within me and does not allow my soul to reign in peace.

4. But *You, who rule the powers of the sea and calm its surging waves*,[7] *rise up and help me*.[8] *Scatter the nations that delight in war*[9] and crush them with Your power.

Show me, I ask You, Your wonderful works and *let Your right hand be glorified*,[10] for You, my Lord God, are my only hope and my sole refuge.

35. *There Is No Freedom from Temptation in This Life*

Jesus:

My son, you are never safe in this life, and as long as you live you will need to be outfitted with spiritual weaponry.

[4]Col. 3:11 [5]Cf. Rom. 6:6 [6]Gal. 5:17 [7]Ps. 89:9
[8]Ps. 44:26 [9]Ps. 68:30 [10]Sir. 36:6

You dwell in the midst of enemies and suffer attacks *on your right and on your left.*[1] Unless you outfit yourself with the *shield of patience*[2] you will soon be wounded.

Furthermore, if you do not fix your heart on Me and sincerely desire to suffer all things for Me, you will not be able to withstand the fierceness of the battle nor attain the crown reserved for the blessed. Therefore, you must bear all things manfully and use a strong arm against your enemies.

Heavenly manna is granted the victor,[3] but much misery is reserved for the sluggard.

2. If you look for rest in this life, how will you ever arrive at eternal rest? Don't make rest your present goal, make it stalwart patience.

Seek true peace, not here on earth but in heaven; seek it not among men nor among other creatures, but in God alone.

You must be willing, for the love of God, to endure all things, for example, labor and sorrow, temptation and annoyance, anxiety and want, illness and injury, opposition and reproach, humiliation and disgrace, censure and contempt. All these will help you to acquire virtue. While they test him who has only begun to follow Christ, they also fashion his heavenly crown.

For a short stint at work, I offer eternal rest, and for enduring a short season of shame, I offer infinite glory.

3. Do you think you will always enjoy spiritual consolation and have it whenever you desire it?

My saints did not always have it, in fact, they endured various trials, a good many temptations, and frequent desolation. Nevertheless, with patience they lived through all this and manifested greater confidence in God than in themselves.

[1] 2 Cor. 6:7 [2] Ps. 91:4 [3] Rev. 2:17

They realized that *the suffering of this life could not be compared to the glory that is to come.*[4]

Do you wish to obtain all at once what many only received with difficulty and only after shedding many tears and sustaining overwhelming labors? *Wait for the Lord, be strong, and show courage.*[5] Don't lose heart, and don't give in to despondency; instead, continually risk your body and soul for God's glory. I will, in turn, reward you most abundantly and *I will be with you in your every trial.*[6]

36. *Against the Vain Judgments of Men*

Jesus:

My son, cast yourself firmly on to the Lord with all your heart and, if your conscience witnesses to your innocence and devotion, then do not fear the judgments that men may speak against you.

It is both profitable and holy to suffer such remarks, and this will not be difficult to him whose heart is humble and whose trust is in God rather than in himself. There are many who talk overmuch, and as a result only a few men pay them any attention. Remember, you cannot satisfy everyone.

Though St. Paul attempted *to please everyone in the Lord*[1] and *became all things to all men,*[2] nevertheless, *he considered it a trifling matter to be judged by men.*[3]

2. With all the talent and power that was his, St. Paul strenuously labored for the salvation and spiritual upbringing of all his hearers; still this did not keep him from being judged or from being despised by them.

[4]Rom. 8:18 [5]Ps. 27:14 [6]Ps. 91:15
[1]1 Cor. 10:33 [2]1 Cor. 9:22 [3]1 Cor. 4:3

He committed everything to God, who knows all things, and humbly and patiently defended himself against those who spoke evil of him, who considered him foolish, who spread lies and hurled all kinds of insults against him. He sometimes, however, did respond to their accusations[4] only so that the weak should not be led astray by his silence.

3. *Who are you that you should be afraid of mortal man?*[5] *Today man is here, but tomorrow he will no longer be found.*[6] Fear only God and the terrors of men will not frighten you.

What can another's words or another's wrongdoings do to you? The one who speaks such words inflicts more harm on himself than on you, and *no matter who he is he cannot escape God's judgment.*[7]

Keep God before your eyes and do not respond to these men with fighting words.[8] If, for the present, you should be overcome and suffer undeserved defeat, don't complain nor manifest any impatience that can lessen your heavenly crown, but raise your eyes to Me in heaven, for I can deliver you from every disgrace and wrong, and *repay each one according to his works.*[9]

37. *Total Self-Surrender Means Full Freedom of Heart*

Jesus:

My son, if you lose yourself you will find Me. Renounce your will and your possessions and you will be the one who gains thereby. As soon as you resign yourself to Me and never

[4]Cf. Acts 26:1 [5]Is. 51:12 [6]1 Macc. 2:63 [7]Rom. 2:3
[8]Cf. 2 Tim. 2:14 [9]Rom. 2:6

withdraw your resolve, greater graces will be yours.

Disciple:

Lord, how often should I resign myself and what should I renounce?

Jesus:

Always and at all times; small things as well as great ones. I make no exceptions. I want to find you stripped naked of everything. Unless you outwardly and inwardly divest yourself of your will, how can you be Mine, or how can I be yours?

The sooner you do this, the better off you will be. The more sincerely and the more completely you put this into practice, so much the more will you please Me, and so much the greater the gain that will be yours.

2. Some people make this resignation of themselves but at the same time they attach one or two conditions. These people do not have full trust in God and so they seek to provide for themselves. And there are some who at the beginning do fully resign themselves, but later on, tired by temptation, they take back what they had previously renounced and as a result make no progress in attaining virtue.

Unless these people unconditionally surrender themselves and daily offer themselves as a sacrifice to Me, they will never achieve the true freedom of a pure heart, nor will they obtain the grace of a delightful familiarity with Me. Without such a self-surrender there can never be a happy and joyful union between us.

3. I have often told you and I again repeat it: Resign yourself, renounce yourself, then you will enjoy great interior peace. Give all for all, seek nothing in return and take nothing back. Remain unflinchingly in Me and you will have Me. You

will then be free in heart and *no darkness will overshadow you.*[1]

Let this be the goal of your striving and the object of your prayer, namely, to desire to be stripped of all your belongings, and once naked, that you may be ready to follow the naked Jesus. You must die to yourself to live eternally with Me.

All your foolish imaginings will disappear, as well as the evil thoughts and useless worries that plague you. All unreasonable fear will depart from you and all unregulated love will die in you.

38. *Keeping Good Order in Our Actions and Having Recourse to God in Time of Danger*

Jesus:

My son, you must diligently see to it that wherever you are and in whatever you do — I refer to your external actions — you are interiorly free and act as your own master, that is, everything should be subject to you and you should be subject to nothing.

You are to be lord and master of your actions and not their slave nor hired servant. You are to be a true Israelite, redeemed from captivity and enjoying the *glorious liberty of the children of God.*[1]

You must keep your head above the contingencies of the present and contemplate the eternal. Look on ephemeral things with one eye and with the other gaze upon celestial things.

Don't allow temporal things to so attract you that you find yourself clinging to them, but use them for your spiritual

[1]Ps. 139:11

[1]Rom. 8:21

advantage as God, the Supreme Maker, who has left nothing disordered in His creation, has designed and ordained them.

2. No matter what the occasion or the event, do not judge it according to mere outward appearances, nor interpret all that you see and hear with your body's eye. But in every instance enter with Moses into the Tabernacle and consult the Lord,[2] and you will frequently receive the divine response that enables you to return informed about present and future events.

Whenever Moses had doubts to be solved or questions that needed answers he went into the Tabernacle, but he likewise went there in order to pray, for example, to avert some calamity or to free himself from other men's wickedness. You should also enter the innermost chamber of your heart and there earnestly beg divine aid.

We read how Joshua and the children of Israel, because they did not first consult the Lord, were deceived by the Gibeonites;[3] much too readily did they believe sweet-sounding words and thus they were duped into falling for a fictitious piety.

39. *Not Becoming Overly Anxious in Our Affairs*

Jesus:

Son, always bring your problems to Me and I will solve them at their proper time. Wait for My answer and you will find that everything will work for your benefit.

[2]Cf. Ex. 33:8 [3]Cf. Josh. 9:14

Disciple:

Most willingly, Lord, do I bring everything before You, for my own thinking on these matters benefits me very little. I wish I had not dwelt so much on future events and had offered myself unhesitatingly to Your good will.

Jesus:

2. My son, it often happens that a man sedulously pursues what he desires, but when he finally obtains it he finds that he feels differently about it. A man's inclinations do not always remain the same; at one given moment he is driven toward one object, and at another he is impelled toward some other object. It is important, therefore, for you to renounce yourself even in the smallest of matters.

3. A man's spiritual progress lies in the denying of himself, and the man who has renounced himself is the man who is most free and enjoys the greatest security.

The old enemy, the devil[1] who opposes everything good, never stops his tempting, and day and night he hatches his nefarious plots, hoping to deceive some unsuspecting individual and bring him to ruin. *Watch and pray, therefore, that you enter not into temptation.*[2]

40. *Man Has No Goodness in Himself and Has No Reason for Boasting*

Disciple:

Lord, what is man that You are mindful of him, and the son of man that You visit him?[1] If You forsake me, Lord, I have no

[1] 1 Pet. 5:8 [2] Matt. 26:41 [1] Ps. 8:4

reason to complain, and if You refuse to answer my petition I have no cause to grumble.

But, surely, this I can think and say: Lord, I am nothing and can do nothing! There is no good in me; I am much less than I should be, and I lean toward nothingness. Unless Your help comes to me and I am interiorly taught by You, I can only grow lax and cool.

2. *You, Lord, however, are always the same and will remain so forever.*[2] You are always good, just, and holy, and all your actions are carried out with the same goodness, justice, and holiness, for all things have been ordained wisely.

I, who am more disposed to go backward than to go forward, do not always remain in the same state, but change as every individual does when the seven ages of man[3] come upon him.

Nevertheless, everything will improve when it pleases You to stretch forth Your helping hand, for You alone, and without any human aid, can assist me, and so powerfully can You strengthen me that *my countenance will no longer be sad*[4] and my heart will turn to You and rest in You alone.

3. If I knew how to set aside all human comforts, either for the sake of increasing my devotion or because I felt impelled to seek You — *there is no man who can comfort me*[5] — then I might rightly hope for Your grace and again rejoice in Your new gift of consolation.

4. Whenever it goes well with me, I offer my thanks to You from whom everything comes. *In Your sight I am worthless and nothing,*[6] a feeble and fickle individual.

What have I to boast about or why do I desire to be esteemed by others? Should I be esteemed because of my

[2]Ps. 102:27 [3]Cf. Dan. 4:16 [4]1 Sam. 1:18 [5]Lam. 1:2
[6]Ps. 39:5

nothingness? This would indeed be the height of folly.

Vainglory is a pernicious plague and the pinnacle of pride since it draws a man away from true glory and robs him of heaven's grace. As long as a man is pleased with himself he is displeasing to God, and as long as he seeks human praise he deprives himself of true virtue.

5. True glory and holy joy are found in glorifying You and not in boasting about myself; in rejoicing in Your name and not in my own strength nor taking delight in any creature but only in You.

May Your name be praised, not mine; may Your works be extolled, not mine. May Your holy name be blessed, and never let the praise of other men come near me. You are my glory and the joy of my heart. In You I glory and *exult all the day long.*[7] *But as for myself, I boast in nothing except my weaknesses.*[8]

6. Let others *seek the glory that comes from other men, but I will seek the glory that comes from the only God.*[9] All human glory, all temporal honor, all worldly acclaim, when compared to Your eternal glory, is but stupid foolishness.

My God, Blessed Trinity, my Truth and my Mercy, to You alone be praise, honor, power, and glory for age after endless age.

41. *Despising the World's Honors*

Jesus:

My son, don't feel down in the dumps when you see others being promoted and receiving honors, while you are being humiliated and overlooked. Raise your heart to Me in heaven

[7]Ps. 89:16 [8]2 Cor. 12:5 [9]John 5:44

and the disdain that the world shows you will no longer grieve you.

Disciple:

Lord, I live in a world full of blindness and am the easy victim of vanity. If I review my life with some care I discover that no creature has ever wronged me and, hence, I really have no reason to bring any complaint against You.

2. Because I have often sinned against You, and seriously too, all creation has rightly taken up arms against me. Justly I deserve shame and contempt, but You deserve praise, honor, and glory.

Unless I prepare myself and am willing to have everyone despise and ignore me, and be looked upon as a mere nobody, only then can I win interior peace for myself. Only then can I become spiritually enlightened and enjoy full union with You.

42. *Our Peace Does Not Depend on Men*

Jesus:

My son, if your peace is founded on some individual who is likeable and whose company you enjoy, you will always be restless and find yourself ensnared. But if you turn to the ever living and everlasting Truth, you will not be saddened when a friend leaves you or when a friend must die.

Your love for your friend has to be rooted in Me, and no matter how good he appears to be, or how very dear he is to you, he should be loved for My sake.

Without Me all friendship is valueless and will not last long. If I am not the bond that unites you in love, then it is neither a true nor pure love.[1]

Your affection toward your friend ought to be so disciplined that, as far as it rests with you, you would prefer to be without all human companionship. The nearer a man approaches God, the Father, to that degree does he withdraw from earthly consolations; and the deeper he descends within himself and the more radically he despises himself, the higher is his ascent to God.

2. The man who attributes anything good to himself keeps God's grace from flowing into him, for *the grace of the Holy Spirit always seeks a humble heart.*[2]

If you knew how to reduce yourself to utter nothingness and liberate yourself from all created love, how I would then inundate your heart with My grace!

If you have eyes only for creatures then you will lose sight of God's face. Learn, therefore, to conquer yourself in all things and you will come to possess divine knowledge.

Whenever you love anything inordinately, no matter how tiny it may be, it still holds you back from your Supreme Good and can only bring harm to your soul.

43. *Against Useless and Worldly Learning*

Jesus:

My son, don't let the fine phrases and subtle speech of other men influence you for *the kingdom of God does not consist in words but in power.*[1] Listen to My words for it is these that enkindle the heart and enlighten the mind, excite repentance and effect much consolation.

[1]Cf. Augustine, *Confessions* IV, 4 [2]1 Pet. 5:5 [1]1 Cor. 4:20

Never read anything with the intention of appearing educated and erudite, rather, learn how to eradicate your evil ways. This will be of greater profit to you than knowing the answers to many abstruse questions.

2. When you have read a great deal and have gained much information about a variety of subjects, you must always return to this basic principle: It is *I who give knowledge to men,*[2] and it is *I who give My little ones an understanding of things*[3] that is clearer than what they could possibly receive from men.

The man who listens to My words becomes wise before long, and makes great progress in the spiritual life, but woe to those who seek useless bits of trivia and care little about knowing how to serve Me.

The time is coming *when Christ,* the teacher of teachers and lord of angels, *will appear*[4] to inspect everyone's homework, that is, to examine each one's conscience. On that day *He will search all Jerusalem with a lamp;*[5] *He will bring to light the things that are now hidden in darkness*[6] and will silence the tongues of quarrelsome men.

I am He who, in an instant, can raise up the humble man's mind to a better understanding of the principles of eternal truth than if he had spent ten years studying them at a university.

When I teach, I use neither words nor sounds. I teach without confusing minds, without encouraging a desire for honors, and without conflicting arguments.

I am He who teaches you to despise the things of the world, to loathe the transitory and seek the heavenly, to relish the eternal and flee earthly honors, to suffer humiliation and to put all your trust in Me, to desire nothing apart from Me and

[2]Ps. 94:10 [3]Ps. 119:130 [4]Col. 3:4 [5]Zeph. 1:12 [6]1 Cor 4:5

to burn with a love for Me that is above all else.

3. Once there was a certain individual who had great love for Me and learned the divine truths directly from Me and preached most eloquently about Me.[7] He made greater progress by his renunciation of everything than he could have by sedulously studying scholastic subtleties.

To some I teach what is meant for all men, and to others I teach what is for them alone. To some I make Myself known by means of suitable signs and figures, and to others I reveal My mysteries in all their brightness.

A book has but a single lesson but everyone who reads it does not profit from it in the same way, for I am the interior teacher of truth and the reader of men's hearts. I understand each one's thoughts and I encourage their actions, *apportioning to each one as I see fit.*[8]

44. *Avoid Being Drawn into External Affairs*

Jesus:

My son, in many matters you must remain ignorant and think of yourself as someone dead on earth, and as one *to whom the whole world is crucified.*[1] You must go about with your ears closed to the world for it is much better for you to spend your time thinking of what is more for your peace.

It is better for you to avert your eyes from what displeases you and to leave each one to his own opinion than to enter into contentious controversy. If you maintain a proper relationship with God and respect His judgment of things, the

[7]This individual remains unidentified; however, some see this as a reference to St. Anthony of Padua (1195-1231).

[8]1 Cor. 12:1 [1]Gal. 6:14

more easily will you bear it when others gain the victory over you.

Disciple:

2. O Lord, to what have we come? We mourn our temporal losses and for a trifling gain we work long hours and dash about every which way. We are totally unmindful of the injury it causes our spiritual life, and later on we rarely even think about it.

We devote much of our time to what is inconsequential and insignificant and neglect that which is of the greatest importance to us. Unless the man, who gives himself entirely to external affairs, returns to his senses, and quickly too, he will soon find himself snugly settled in the web of earthly affairs.

45. *Not Everyone Should Be Believed and How Easy It Is To Offend by Words*

Disciple:

Lord, send me your help in this time of trial *for useless is the help that comes from man.*[1] How often I have found no loyalty where I had hoped to find it, and how often I have discovered it where I had least expected it! It is foolish, therefore, to put your trust in men; *the just man's salvation is in You, O God.*[2]

My Lord God, may You be blessed in everything that happens to us. We are without strength and by ourselves we stagger; we are quick to make mistakes and quick to undergo change.

[1]Ps. 60:11 [2]Ps. 37:39

2. Is there anyone so careful and cautious in his every action that he never falls into error or doubt? The one who trusts in You, Lord, and *seeks You with all his heart*[3] does not readily fall.

If he should, however, fall into some kind of trouble — no matter how entangled he has become — You will quickly rescue him or console him for You never abandon those who trust in You unto the end.

3. Rare is the friend who faithfully stands by another friend in all his trials. Lord, You alone are most faithful in everything. There is no one as loyal as You.

What great wisdom that holy soul had who said: *My mind is firmly established and grounded in Christ.*[4] If I were of this same opinion I would fear no man and no man's sharp words could ever hurt me.

4. Who can foresee everything that is to happen, or who can take precautions against all future misfortunes? If the things we do foresee bring us harm, what about unforeseen calamities? Surely they will afflict us most grievously.

Why did I not make better provision for my wretched self? Why was I so ready to put my trust in other men? We are mere human beings, nothing more than weak men, notwithstanding that many do consider us angels and even call us by that name.

Lord, whom shall I trust? No one but You! *You are the Truth;*[5] and You can neither deceive nor be deceived.

Furthermore, *every man is false,*[6] feeble, unsteady, and

[3]Wis. 1:1

[4]This statement is attributed to St. Agatha (+ ca. 250) in the Acts of her martyrdom.

[5]John 14:6 [6]Rom. 3:4

especially fickle in his speech, and he should scarcely be believed even though his words may seem to ring true.

5. Wisely have You admonished us *to beware of men,*[7] that *a man's enemies are those of his own household,*[8] and that we *ought not believe it if someone should say "Here he is!" or "Look, there he is!"*[9]

At great expense have I learned my lesson; would that it make me more cautious and not add to my foolishness. Someone once said to me: "Keep this to yourself and don't tell anyone what I have just told you." While I kept silent and regarded the matter between us a secret, the man himself could not keep still about it and he soon betrayed both himself and me and then went his way.

From all such thoughtless people and their gossip, deliver me, Lord, for I don't want to fall into their hands nor do as they do. Let my lips speak only what is true and honest and keep my tongue from all sly speech. What I am unwilling to tolerate in others I must, by all means, avoid doing myself.

6. How wonderful and peaceful a feeling it is when we keep silent about other people and refrain from believing and spreading about all that comes to our ears. We should confide in only a few individuals, but we ought always seek You, Lord, who read our hearts. We ought not let windy words waft us about but ought to desire that everything, both within and outside us, be done in accordance with Your good pleasure.

If we want to preserve heaven's grace in us, we will avoid all external show and not look for public acclaim or people's admiration, but untiringly pursue what helps to amend our life and increase our devotion.

[7]Matt. 10:17 [8]Matt. 10:36 [9]Matt. 24:23

7. Many have been injured because their virtue, once it had become known to others, was prematurely praised; many have, on the other hand, profited by having that grace kept hidden while living this fragile life with its unending series of conflicts and contests.

46. *When Men Direct Sharp Words Against You, Put Your Trust in God*

Jesus:

My son, stand firm and trust in Me. Words, after all, are only words. They dart through the air but they hurt no one; they can't even put a scratch on a stone.

If you are guilty of some wrongdoing, think about willingly correcting yourself, and if you are unaware of any fault on your part, then think about gladly enduring these stinging words for the sake of God.

To put up with a few harsh words now and then is nothing great when you are still incapable of enduring harsh blows.

Why do you make such trifling matters into mountains? Because you still have a worldly outlook and pay more attention to others' opinions than you should. You are afraid that men may ridicule you and hence you are unwilling to be taken to task for your faults, and so you make excuses to cover up your actions.

2. Take a good and thorough look at yourself and you will find that the world still resides in you and that you still foolishly desire to please men. Since you refuse to be taken down from your pedestal and be censured for your wrongdo-

ings, it is obvious that you are not really humble, or dead to the world, nor *is the world crucified to you.*[1]

Pay attention to My words and you will not care about the *ten thousand words*[2] that come from men. If all that human malice could possibly excogitate were uttered against you, what harm could all that do if you just let it pass you by and consider it nothing more than rubbish? All such talk can't do as much as pluck a single strand of hair from your head.[3]

3. The man whose heart is not interiorly recollected and whose eyes are not fixed on God is easily disturbed by words of reproach, but he who trusts in Me and desires not to stand by his own judgment fears no man.

I am the judge and I know all secrets. I know how everything comes to pass and I know who has caused an injury and who has suffered it. All this is in accordance with My will, for whatever occurs happens with My permission so *that the thoughts of many hearts may be revealed.*[4]

I shall be the final judge of both the guilty and the innocent, but I have desired to first try them in My secret court.

4. The testimony of men is often erroneous, but My verdict is always true. It will stand firm and never be reversed. It is hidden from the multitude but manifest to only a few. Though to the unwise it may appear unfair it is not in error nor can it be. Therefore, come to Me with every case that needs judgment and never rely upon your own understanding.

The just man will not be distressed *by whatever happens to him*[5] by God's will. Even if something unjust be said against him, he will not greatly care, nor will he be so idiotic as to rejoice when others with good reason acquit him.

[1]Gal. 6:14 [2]1 Cor. 14:19 [3]Cf. Luke 21:18
[4]Luke 2:35 [5]Prov. 12:21

5. The just man knows that *I read men's minds and hearts*[6] and *I do not judge according to appearances,*[7] nor according to human standards. What is blameworthy in My eyes men often judge as praiseworthy.

Disciple:

Lord God, strong, patient and just Judge, who knows the weakness and perversity in men, be my strength and my confidence, for my own conscience is not enough for me. You know all that I do not know and, therefore, I ought to have humbled myself when I was rebuked and ought to have borne it in meekness.

In Your mercy, pardon me for all the times that I have not acted so in the past and give me the grace to endure still more in the future. Better for me is Your abundant mercy and its pardon than any self-defense stemming from a presumed righteousness on my part.

Though I am not aware of anything against myself, I am not thereby acquitted,[8] for if You withhold Your mercy *no living being can stand justified in Your sight.*[9]

47. *Trials Must Be Endured To Gain Eternal Life*

Jesus:

My son, do not let the work you have undertaken for Me wear you down, nor let tribulation dishearten you, but always let My promise strengthen and console you. The reward I offer you is beyond measure and without limit.

[6]Rev. 2:23 [7]John 7:24 [8]1 Cor. 4:4 [9]Ps. 143:2

You will not labor here much longer nor will you always be weighted down with sorrow. Wait but a short time and you will see your trials come to a swift end; the hour will come when all toil and trouble will cease. Everything that passes with time is short-lived and of little consequence.

2. Do well whatever you are doing; work faithfully in My vineyard and I will be your reward.[1] Continue with your reading or writing, singing or mourning; keep silent, pray and endure all trials as a man should. Eternal life is worth these and even greater conflicts.

Peace will come on a day known only to the Lord and it will not be a day or night such as we now experience, but it will be a day of unending light, of infinite brightness, of everlasting peace and enduring rest.

On that day you will not say: *Who will deliver me from this body of death?*[2] Nor will you cry out: *Woe to me for sojourning here for so long a time.*[3] *Death will be overthrown,*[4] and salvation assured forever. There will be no more anxiety but only blessed joy in the sweet and lovely fellowship of our being together.

3. If only you had seen the everlasting crowns of the saints in heaven and the great glory they now enjoy! What a difference, from the time they were on earth where they were treated as objects of contempt and were considered unfit to live. If you had seen their crowns and glory you would have immediately humbled yourself to the very earth and sought to be everyone's servant rather than to be lord over a single individual.

You would not look forward to joy-filled days in this life but you would find greater happiness in suffering for God, and

[1]Cf. Matt. 20:4, 7 [2]Rom. 7:24 [3]Ps. 120:5 [4]Is. 25:8

you would account it your greatest blessing to be reckoned as nothing among men.

4. O, if you found relish in these thoughts and allowed them to penetrate your heart, you would never dare to let slip a single word of complaint.

Are not all arduous labors to be endured to gain eternal life? Losing or gaining the kingdom of God is no small matter!

Turn your face toward Me in heaven where I reside with My saints who had *endured hard struggles*[5] in the world and now live amid joy and consolation. They are now secure and are at rest and *will remain with Me in My Father's kingdom*[6] for all eternity.

48. *The Day of Eternity and the Trials of This Life*

Disciple:

O most blessed mansion of the celestial city! O splendor-filled day of eternity, never obscured by night and ever radiating the Supreme Truth! O day, always joyful, always assured, and never changing into darkness!

Would that that day had already dawned and all these time-bound things had come to an end! That day, resplendent with everlasting brightness, now shines on the saints, but for us *who are still on our pilgrimage on earth*[1] it is seen only from afar and *as through a dark glass.*[2]

2. The citizens of heaven know how joyful that day is, but

[5]Heb. 10:32 [6]Matt. 26:29
[1]Heb. 11:13 [2]1 Cor. 13:12

we, *poor banished children of Eve,*[3] mourn our day filled as it is with bitterness and weariness.

The days of this life are but few and evil,[4] filled with sorrow and misery. Here a man is tainted by many sins, ensnared by many passions, held down by many fears, surrounded by many cares, distracted by many curiosities, entangled in much foolishness, encompassed by many errors, worn out by many labors, troubled by many temptations, weakened by many pleasures, and tormented by want.

3. When will there be an end to all these evils? When will I be set free from sin's wretched slavery?

When, Lord, will I think of You alone? When will I fully rejoice in You?

When will I be truly free with nothing to hold me back and with no distress of mind and body?

When will there be a stable peace, a secure and undisturbed peace, a peace within me and around me, a peace assured in every way?

When, good Jesus, will I stand in Your presence and see You? When will I contemplate the glory of Your kingdom? When *will You be all in all to me*?[5]

When will I be with You *in the kingdom You have prepared from all eternity for those who love You*?[6]

I am but a poor abandoned exile in a hostile land where daily wars and grievous misfortunes encircle me.

4. Console me in my banishment; soothe away my sorrow for my every desire is to seek You. All that this world offers me in the way of comfort is really burdensome.

I want to enjoy You deep within me, but I cannot attain it. I desire to hold fast to heavenly things but temporal realities and

[3]*Salve Regina* [4]Gen. 47:9 [5]Col. 3:11 [6]Matt. 25:34

my unmortified passions weigh me down. With my mind I wish to rise over and above all things, but my body compels me, unwilling as I am, to be its servant.

How unfortunate a man am I! I struggle against myself and am a burden to myself, and while my spirit desires to soar above, my flesh pulls me downward.

5. How I suffer within me! When I try to think of heavenly things a crowd of carnal thoughts forces its way into my prayers. *Be not far from me, my God,*[7] nor *turn away in anger from Your servant.*[8] *Flash forth Your lightning and scatter them, send out Your arrows*[9] and dissipate these thoughts introduced by my enemy.

Fix all my senses on You, make me forget all worldly things and help me speedily to reject and despise all sinful imaginings. Eternal Truth, come to my aid so that no vanity may ever entice me. Come, heavenly Sweetness, so that all that is impure may flee before Your face.

Pardon me, and mercifully forgive me for the times I have dwelt on things other than You during prayer. Truly, I confess that I have been in the habit of yielding to distractions. Many times I am not where my body may be sitting or standing, but am where my thoughts have carried me. I am where my thoughts are, and my thoughts are usually with the things I love. What quickly enters my thoughts is what is naturally delightful, or what has become pleasurable by constant use.

6. You, who are Truth, have plainly said: *Where your treasure is there will your heart also be!*[10]

If I love heaven, I gladly think of heavenly things. If I love the world, I rejoice in worldly pleasures and am saddened by its woes.

[7]Ps. 71:12 [8]Ps. 27:9 [9]Ps. 144:6 [10]Matt. 6:21

If I love the body, my imagination is always on things of the flesh. If I love the spirit, I delight in thinking about spiritual matters.

Whatever it is that I love, I eagerly speak of it and enjoy hearing about it, and I carry its mental image home within me.

Blessed is that man who, for Your sake, Lord, renounces creatures, does violence to his nature and, because of the great fervor within him, *crucifies his flesh with all its passions and lusts.*[11] Now that his conscience is serene and tranquil he may offer You unblemished prayer and having shut out all worldly things, not only within him but likewise all those outside him, he is worthy to be numbered among those in the angelic choir.

49. *The Desire for Eternal Life and the Great Blessings Promised to Those Who Strive for It*

Jesus:

My son, when you feel the desire for eternal happiness take hold of you from above, and when you long to be free of your body's dwelling in order to contemplate *my never-diminishing glory,*[1] open wide your heart and fervently accept this holy inspiration of Mine.

Offer your most heartfelt thanks to the Divine Goodness who treats you so generously, who visits you with mercy, who encourages you so robustly, and mightily raises you up so that you may not fall, because of your weight, and again be bogged down amid the things of earth.

You receive these gifts not because of your way of thinking or because of any exertion on your part, but solely through the

[11]Gal. 5:24 [1]James 1:17

good favor of heaven's grace and the divine regard, so that you may grow in virtue, advance in humility, prepare yourself for future struggles, and that you may cling to Me with all your heart and serve Me with a fervent will.

2. My son, when a fire burns, its flames mount upwards but there is always some smoke rising amid them. Similarly, some people have a burning desire for the things of heaven, but they are not yet free of the temptations that come from the flesh, and when these people earnestly offer their prayers to God they do not act purely or solely for God's honor. This is also the case with your own prayers though you persist in considering them most sincere. Any prayer tainted by self-interest is neither pure nor perfect.

3. Don't ask for what is pleasing and helpful to you, but pray for what is acceptable to Me and for what gives Me honor. If you view things in their proper light you will prefer to follow My commands rather than your desires.

I know your desires and I have heard your frequent prayers. You would like to enjoy *the glorious liberty of the children of God*[2] living in your eternal home in the heavenly fatherland. But that hour has not yet come; you are still in another time zone, namely in the time of war, the time for work and woe.

You wish to be filled with the Supreme Good, but you cannot attain to it at present. I am that Supreme Good. Wait for me, says the Lord, *until the kingdom of God comes.*[3]

4. You must still undergo more testing on earth and be tried in many more trials. Consolation will sometimes be yours, but not in its fullness. *Be strong and of good courage,*[4] doing and enduring all that goes contrary to nature.

You must *put on the new man*[5] and be transformed into

[2]Rom. 8:21 [3]Luke 22:18 [4]Josh. 1:6 [5]Eph. 4:24

someone else. Often you must do what you do not want to do, and what you want to do you must set aside.

Other people's affairs will meet with success but your desires will meet with failure.

Others will speak and they will be listened to, but what you say will be taken as nothing.

Others will make requests and they will receive, but what you ask for will go unanswered.

5. Others will be praised by men, but you will be passed over in silence.

Others will meet with advancement but you will be overlooked as a good-for-nothing. All this will naturally upset you but it will be to your great spiritual advantage to bear it and to do so in silence.

In these and similar ways the faithful servant of God is accustomed to being tried to see to what degree he can renounce himself and how well he can break his stubborn will.

There is hardly anything in which we have such need to die to self as in seeing and suffering things that go contrary to our will, especially when we are commanded to do what appears to us to be useless or absurd. Since we are under obedience we dare not oppose someone in higher authority, and so it becomes quite difficult for us to respond to another's every beck and call and forget our own views in the matter.

6. My son, look at the fruit of your labors. When you think of how quickly they will come to an end, and of the exceedingly great reward that will be yours, you will no longer look upon them as a source of grief but as the consoling consequence of your patience.

In exchange for sacrificing the little choice you had, your will will always be fulfilled in heaven.

There you will find all that you wish, and all that you can desire.

There you will possess all goodness without fear of ever losing it.

There your will will be one with Mine and never will it desire anything that is selfish or anything that is not I.

There no one will oppose you, and no one will complain about you. There no one will hinder you, or stand in your way. There all your desires will be together, all satisfied and all filled to overflowing.

There I will give you glory for the insults you sustained, a *mantle of praise*[6] to replace your sorrow, and for the lowest place that was yours on earth, I offer you a throne in the eternal kingdom.

There the fruitfulness of your obedience will be made manifest to everyone; your acts of penance will be transformed into joy, and the humble subjection of yourself will receive its crown of glory.

7. Therefore, bow your head in humility and place yourself in another's hands, and think not of the person who is asking you to do this or is ordering you to do that. This should be your prime concern, whether a superior, an inferior, or an equal asks or suggests something of you, take it all in good part and show your good will by promptly performing it.

Let one individual seek one thing and let someone else desire another; let one find glory in one deed and another find it in something else. And let them all be praised thousands and thousands of times, but as for you, you are to rejoice in none of

[6]Is. 61:3

these but only in despising yourself and in following My good pleasure and honor.

Let this be your only desire, that *God may always be glorified in you, whether by life or by death.*[7]

50. *The Desolate Man Should Place Himself in God's Hands*

Disciple:

Lord God, holy Father, may You be blessed now and forever! As You will it, so it is, and all that You do is good. Let Your servant find his joy in You and not in himself or in anything else. You alone, Lord, are the true joy; You alone are my hope and my crown, my happiness and my honor.

What does Your servant have that he has not received[1] from You, and without meriting any of it? All that You have made and all that You have given me is Yours. Everything is Yours!

I am wretched and *have been afflicted since my early youth.*[2] Sometimes my soul is sad even to the point of shedding tears and it is often troubled because of trials that threaten.

2. I look for the joy of Your peace. I fervently pray for the peace that belongs to Your children whom you nourish with the light of Your consolation.

If You grant me this peace and pour Your holy joy into my soul, I will be filled with music and wholeheartedly will I sing out Your praises. But if You take Yourself from me, as You often do, I will find it difficult to walk *the pathways of Your commandments.*[3] I will fall on my knees and strike my breast

[7]Phil. 1:20 [1]1 Cor. 4:7 [2]Ps. 88:15 [3]Ps. 119:35

bewailing that today is not as fine a day as yesterday or the day before *when Your lamp kept shining on my head,*[4] and when I found, *in the shadow of Your wings,*[5] protection from temptation's assaults.

3. Father, all just and worthy of everlasting praise, the hour has come for Your servant to be tested.

Father, worthy of all love, it is only right that at this hour I should suffer something for Your sake.

Father, worthy of endless honor, the hour is now here which You foresaw from all eternity when I, Your servant, should be struck down and for a time be overwhelmed though, through it all, I continually live in Your presence. For a short period I am to be ridiculed, rebuked, and have my reputation ruined; I am to be worn out by weariness and sufferings, only that I may rise again with You at the dawn of the new day and receive heaven's glory.

Father, all holy, this is the way You have designed it and desired it and since You have commanded it, it has come to pass.

4. This is the grace You grant Your friends: to suffer and endure distress in this world for love of You — as often as You allow it and only from sources You permit. Nothing happens on earth without Your wisdom and providence, and nothing ever happens without good reason.

It is good, Lord, that You have humbled me so that I may learn Your justifications,[6] and that I may cast from me all pride and presumption of heart. It is for my own good *that shame has covered my face*[7] and that I seek my consolation in You rather than in men. From this I have also learned that I am to reverence Your unsearchable judgments which affect both the

[4]Job 29:3 [5]Ps. 17:8 [6]Ps. 119:71 [7]Ps. 69:7

good and the bad, but always with justice and equity.

5. I thank You for not having spared me for my sins and for having punished me with bitter stripes. I thank You for inflicting pain on me and for sending me trials that assail me within and without.

Under the heavens there is no one who can console me except You, my Lord God, heavenly physician of souls. *You wound and You heal;*[8] *You take down to the depths but You also raise up.*[9] Your discipline corrects me and Your very rod is my teacher.

6. Beloved Father, *I am in Your hands*[10] and I bend my body to Your correcting rod. Strike me across the back and neck so that I can twist my crookedness into something straight and in accord with Your will. Make me a holy and humble disciple as You have done to others, for I wish to walk in line with Your least desire. To Your correction I give myself and all that is mine. It is better to be punished in this life than in the one to come.

You know each and every single thing,[11] and there is nothing in man's conscience that escapes You. You know the future before it happens and need no one to tell You or to inform You about what is happening on earth.

You know what I need for my spiritual progress and You know how effectively trials serve to scrub away the rust of sin. Do with me as Your good pleasure wills and do not disdain my sinful life which is better and more clearly known to You than to anyone else.

7. Grant me, Lord, to know what I ought to know, to love what I ought to love, and to praise what pleases You the most. Let me hold in esteem what is most precious to You and detest

[8]Deut. 32:39 [9]1 Sam. 2:6 [10]Ps. 31:15 [11]John 16:30

all that is foul in Your sight.

Let me *not judge according to what my eyes see nor decide according to what my ears hear*[12] from ignorant men, but let me, with true judgment, discern between matters material and spiritual, and always and above all seek Your good will and pleasure.

8. Our senses often lead us into making erroneous judgments, and the worldly minded are likewise deceived because their only love is the world.

Is a man any better because other men think him better? When one man praises another it is like a liar speaking to a liar, or a flatterer congratulating a flatterer, or a blind man leading a blind man, or someone feeble giving a helping hand to someone equally feeble. So pointless is this praise that it only brings shame on the individual who falls for it.

The humble St. Francis said: "A man is only as great as he is in Your eyes and no greater."[13]

51. Performing Humble Tasks when Unable To Undertake Higher Ones

Jesus:

My son, you will not always be able to maintain the high level of your burning desire for perfection, nor always remain in the same degree of lofty contemplation. Because of original sin's corruption, you will sometimes have to descend to lesser things, and though you be unwilling and find it annoying, you will have to bear the burden of living in this corruptible life.

[12]Is.11:3 [13]St. Bonaventure, *Major Life of St. Francis,* chap. 6

As long as you are in this mortal body of yours, you will know weariness and heaviness of heart. Therefore, while in the body, you will bemoan the weight of that flesh for it will prevent you from devoting yourself unreservedly to spiritual matters and to divine contemplation.

2. When this happens, it would be better for you to busy yourself in humble outward tasks so that, by doing good works, you can refresh your spirit. Likewise, you should firmly look forward to My coming and visiting you but, in the meantime, patiently bear your exile and suffer the dryness of spirit until I come to you and free you from all your anxieties.

I will make you forget your troubles and you, in turn, will enjoy interior peace. I will spread out before you the gracious grazing grounds of the Scriptures where, with open heart, *you will run in the way of my commandments.*[1] You will then say: *The sufferings of this time are not worth comparing with the future glory that is to be revealed in us.*[2]

52. *Man Deserves Chastisement and Not Consolation*

Disciple:

Lord, I am not worthy of Your consolation nor any spiritual visitation, and when You leave me poor and desolate You treat me only as I deserve.

Even if I were to shed a sea of tears, I would still be unworthy of Your consolation. I deserve nothing but to be flogged and punished for I have often and grievously offended

[1]Ps. 119:32 [2]Rom. 8:18

You and in many ways greatly sinned against You. Therefore, according to all right reason, I am not worthy of Your least consolation.

Merciful and loving God, who do not wish to see Your creatures perish and desire *to manifest the riches of Your goodness toward the vessels of Your mercy,*[1] You deign to console me, Your servant, above all measure and beyond all my deserts. Your consolation, Lord, is so unlike the petty palaver of men!

2. Lord, what have I done for You to give me consolation from heaven? I don't remember doing anything good, I who am at all times inclined to evil and most remiss in reforming my life. What I say is the truth and I am unable to deny it. If I were to speak otherwise, You would challenge me and there would be no one to defend me. What have I deserved for my sins if not hell and eternal fire?

Indeed, I admit that I deserve all scorn and contempt and do not deserve to be counted among Your devoted ones. Though it grieves me to hear this still, for truth's sake, I acknowledge my wrongdoings so that I may the more easily petition Your mercy.

3. What else can I say, guilty as I am and overcome with shame? I can say nothing but this: I have sinned, Lord, I have sinned; have mercy on me and forgive me. Give me a short while to lament my sorrow *before I go to the land that is dark and overcast with death's mist.*[2]

Why do You especially enjoin the guilty and wretched sinner to be filled with sorrow and to humble himself for his wrongdoings? Because from solid contrition and true humility of heart there is born in man the hope for forgiveness; peace returns to the troubled conscience; grace once lost is restored;

[1]Rom. 9:23 [2]Job 10:21

and protection is offered from the wrath to come. In contrition and humility of heart God and the repentant soul meet in a most holy embrace.

4. *Humble sorrow for sins is a sacrifice acceptable to You, Lord,*[3] a sacrifice much sweeter in Your sight than the fragrance rising from burning incense. It is also the soothing ointment You once desired poured on Your sacred feet[4] *for You have never despised a contrite and humble heart.*[5]

It is at Your feet that we have a place of refuge from the raging enemy, and it is there that our brokenness is mended and our uncleanness washed away.

53. *God's Grace Is Not Granted to the Worldly Minded*

Jesus:

Son, My grace is precious and it allows no intermingling with worldly affairs or earthly comforts. If you desire this grace, you must remove every obstacle to receiving it.

Choose some quiet place for yourself and love to dwell there alone. Don't look for occasions for idle conversation, but pour out your devout prayers to God so that you may continue to preserve contrition in your heart and maintain an unblemished conscience.

Look upon the whole world as nothing and prefer serving God to everything else. It is impossible for you to serve Me and at the same time take delight in ephemeral things.

Withdraw from your acquaintances and close friends, and

[3]Ps. 51:17 [4]Cf. Luke 7:46 [5]Ps. 51:17

keep your mind detached from all worldly comfort. This is what the apostle Peter meant when he instructed the followers of Christ to regard themselves as *strangers and pilgrims*[1] in the world.

2. Great is the confidence of the man, who is about to die, when he knows that he has no attachment whatever to anything in this world. But a weak individual cannot bear to have his heart detached from everything, nor can the unspiritual man understand the liberty enjoyed by the spiritual man.[2]

When a man sincerely desires to be spiritual he must renounce all his friends, those near and those far away, and must beware of himself most of all.

If you have completely conquered yourself, you will easily conquer all other things. The perfect victory is to triumph over one's self. The man who has so conquered himself that his flesh is now subject to his reason, and his reason, in turn, is obedient to Me in all things, that man, I say, is master of himself and lord of the world.

3. If you wish to rise to this degree of perfection you must manfully begin *to lay the axe to the root*[3] and dig out and destroy all your hidden unregulated inclinations toward self-love and material advantage.

From this one vice of self-love proceed nearly all the other vices that need uprooting, and as soon as self-love is eradicated, great peace and calm will follow.

Because there are only a few who strive to die perfectly to themselves and, thus, rise far above themselves, countless others remain caught in their own webs and their spirits languish in their incapacity to soar on high.

[1]Pet. 2:11 [2]Cf. 1 Cor. 2:14 [3]Matt. 3:10

Whoever wishes to walk freely with Me must put all evil passions and unregulated desires to death and must never cling to any creature through self-love or self-interest.

54. *The Contrary Inclinations of Nature and Grace*

Jesus:

My son, pay careful attention to the inclinations of Nature and Grace, for they move in contrary directions and with so great a subtlety that only the man who is spiritual and interiorly enlightened can discern them.

All men desire what is good[1] and see goodness in their every word and deed, and thus they deceive themselves by the appearance of good.[2]

Nature is cunning and seductive; it ensnares and deceives many and always has itself as its final goal. Grace advances single-mindedly and *abstains from all forms of evil.*[3] It never yields to deception and always acts purely and simply for God's sake in whom it recognizes its final rest.

2. Nature is most unwilling to die to itself, to be restrained or overcome, to be subjugated and made to obey. Grace, however, strives to mortify itself and resists sensuality, wants to be subjugated and desires to be vanquished, does not seek to enjoy its own freedom but loves to be under discipline, does not long to have authority over anyone but only to be, live, and remain under God, and is always willing to *humbly submit itself to every human being for the sake of God.*[4]

[1]Cf. Aristotle, *Nicomachean Ethics* I, 1

[2]Cf. Horace, *The Art of Poetry* v. 25 [3]1 Thes. 5:22 [4]1 Pet. 2:13

Nature operates only for its own interest and weighs what gain it can acquire from others. Grace, on the other hand, seeks not *what is useful and advantageous to itself but what is profitable to many.*[5]

Nature most willingly accepts honors and homage, but Grace faithfully *ascribes all honor and glory to God.*[6]

3. Nature shivers under shame and contempt, while Grace *rejoices in suffering dishonor for the name of Jesus.*[7]

Nature loves leisure and looks to bodily rest, but Grace despises being idle and joyfully looks for something to do.

Nature seeks to possess things that are rare and beautiful and abhors anything common and crude, but Grace enjoys what is simple and humble, does not avoid what is shabby, and does not mind wearing clothes old and tattered.

Nature is interested in temporal things and is elated when it acquires a terrestrial gain, but agonizes over worldly losses and is even deeply hurt by a single slight syllable that comes its way. Grace, however, is interested in what is eternal, does not cling to anything ephemeral, is not grieved by any earthly loss, nor does it become provoked by harsh words, because it has committed its joy and *treasure in heaven where nothing wastes away.*[8]

4. Nature is filled with greed, prefers to receive rather than to give, and is captivated by all that it possesses. Grace, however, is honest and openhanded, shuns selfishness, is content with little, and considers it *more blessed to give than to receive.*[9]

Nature inclines toward creatures and its own body, toward worthless schemes, and much wandering about. Grace, on the

[5] 1 Cor. 10:33 [6] Ps. 29:2 [7] Acts 5:4 [8] Matt. 6:20
[9] Acts 20:35

other hand, draws toward God and perfection, forswears creatures and flees the world, despises the desires of the flesh, keeps travel to a minimum, and blushes when in public.

Nature is happy to accept any and every comfort that comes from the outside and is a delight to its senses, but Grace seeks its comfort only in God and delights in the Supreme Good rather than in anything visible.

5. Nature accomplishes everything for its own gain and profit, does nothing without receiving recompense and in return for its good deeds expects something equal or better, or else praise and patronage, for it wants men to prize its deeds and donations. Grace, however, seeks nothing temporal, asks for no reward other than God Himself, and desires no more of life's necessities than what serves to attain eternal happiness.

6. Nature finds pleasure in having many friends and relatives, glories in family estates and its genealogical trees, caters to those in power, flatters the wealthy, and applauds those whose thinking is similar to its own. Grace, however, *loves even its enemies,*[10] does not boast about having a multitude of friends and puts no store in lineage or ancestral castles unless these foster greater perfection. It prefers the poor to the rich, has greater feeling for the innocent than the powerful, rejoices to be with him who loves the truth than with one who is a fraud, exhorts the good *earnestly to desire the better gifts,*[11] and to become more like the Son of God by the exercise of virtue.

Nature is quick to complain when it finds itself in need and faces troublesome times, but Grace bears poverty with a resolutely calm spirit.

7. Nature makes itself the center of everything, and contends and fights to maintain itself. Grace, however, refers all

[10]Matt. 5:44 [11]1 Cor. 12:31

things to God from whom they have all come, ascribes no good to itself, nor has it the arrogance to presume upon anything of its own. Grace does not argue with anyone, nor does it prefer its opinion over that expressed by others but submits all its understanding and feelings to God's wisdom for divine scrutiny.

Nature hankers to know secrets and to hear the latest news, to be seen in public and enjoy all manner of new sense experiences, desires to be noticed by others and to do whatever results in acclaim and admiration. Grace, on the other hand, cares little about hearing the news and has no interest in trivia, for it knows that all curiosity has its beginning in man's original corruption and that there is nothing new or lasting on this earth. Grace teaches itself to curb the senses, avoid foolish self-adulation and hollow display, and humbly to conceal its praiseworthy and admirable deeds, and let the fruit of all that it has accomplished and learned be profitable to the soul and advance God's praise and honor.

Grace recoils from praise offered itself and its deeds, but insists that only God be blessed in His gifts which He has bestowed out of His pure love.

8. This Grace is a supernatural light, *a special gift of God,*[12] the distinguishing mark of the elect, and the pledge of eternal salvation which raises a man from the things of the earth to love heavenly realities, and transforms the man who has been slave to the flesh into one that is spiritual.

The more Nature is curbed and conquered, so much the more is Grace infused into the soul, and the man who is devoted to the interior life is, by daily visitations, *refashioned according to the image of God.*[13]

[12]Eph. 2:8 [13]Col. 3:10

55. *The Corruption of Nature and the Efficacy of Divine Grace*

Disciple:

My Lord God, You created me in Your own image and likeness; grant me the grace which You have spoken of as being so important and necessary for salvation, namely, the grace to succeed in conquering this most wicked nature of mine that constantly draws me into sin and is leading me to perdition. *In my body I feel the law of sin contradicting the law of my mind*[1] and it leads me, as a captive, to obey my sensuality in many things. Unless You infuse Your most holy grace into my soul and set me on fire, I will be unable to resist its urgings.

2. I need Your grace, that amazing grace, to subdue my nature *ever prone to evil since the days of my youth.*[2] From the time that nature fell and was made corrupt by the sin of Adam, the first man, *the punishments of that offense have passed on to all men.*[3] Now, that nature, which You originally created good and in a righteous state, is acknowledged as feeble and degenerate, for of itself it entices to base and brutish things.

The little strength that nature retains is nothing more than an ember hidden under ashes. It is natural reason itself, and though enveloped by much darkness, it still preserves the power to judge between good and evil and to discern truth from falsehood. It is unable, however, to execute all that it approves since it no longer possesses the full light of truth and its affections are in an ailing state.

3. Hence it is, my God, that *in my inmost self I delight in Your law,*[4] and know that *Your commands are good, holy, and just,*[5] for

[1]Rom. 7:23 [2]Gen. 8:21 [3]Rom. 5:12 [4]Rom. 7:22
[5]Rom. 7:12

they exhort us to avoid sin and everything evil. Nevertheless, *in my flesh I serve the law of sin*[6] and show more obedience to my senses than to reason.

Thus it happens that though *I will to do what is right, I cannot find the strength to achieve it.*[7] Furthermore, though I make many good resolves, I still pull back and fall apart at the slightest resistance, all because I lack Your grace which alone can help my weakness. Indeed, I recognize the way to perfection and I see clearly enough what I ought to do, but crushed under the weight of my own corruption I am unable to get on my feet and go forward.

4. Lord, how absolutely necessary to me is Your grace if I want to begin something good, to continue with it, and then to complete it. *Without Your grace I can do nothing,*[8] but with it strengthening me *I can do all things.*[9]

O true Grace from heaven, without You our personal merits are nothing and our natural endowments worthless. Neither skills nor riches, neither beauty nor strength, neither talent nor eloquence carry any value in Your sight unless grace be joined with them. Nature's gifts are had by both the good and bad, but grace and love is the special gift granted to the elect, and being sealed with it they are considered worthy of eternal life.

This grace is so excellent that without it neither the gift of prophecy, nor the power to work miracles, nor the capacity to engage in the highest forms of speculation has any worth. Not even faith, or hope, or any of the other virtues are acceptable to You without grace and charity.

5. O most blessed Grace, You make the poor in spirit rich in virtue, and those possessing many blessings humble of

[6]Rom. 7:25 [7]Rom. 7:18 [8]John 15:5

heart. Come, descend upon me like the dew in the early morning and fill me with Your consolation lest my soul grow faint through weariness and dryness of mind.

Lord, I pray that *I may find favor in Your sight.*[10] *Your grace is enough for me,*[11] even if I were to receive none of the things that nature desires. Though tempted and tested by many trials, *I will fear no evil because Your grace will be with me.*[12] Your grace is my strength and it affords me counsel and help; it is stronger than all my enemies and wiser than all the wise.

6. Your grace is the mistress of truth, the teacher of discipline, the enlightener of hearts, the comforter of the afflicted, and the refuge of the sorrowing. Your grace banishes sadness, expels fear, nurtures devotion, and breeds tears. Without Your grace, I am but a piece of dry wood — a useless log — fit only to be set aside.

Therefore, "Lord, let Your grace go before me and follow me and make me ever intent on good works. This I ask through Jesus Christ Your Son. Amen."[13]

56. *Self-Abnegation and Imitating Christ by the Way of the Cross*

Jesus:

My son, to the degree that you can leave yourself behind, to that degree will you be able to enter into Me. Just as desiring nothing outside you produces internal peace within you, so the internal renunciation of yourself unites you to God.

[9]Phil. 4:13 [10]Gen. 18:3 [11]2 Cor. 12:9 [12]Ps. 23:4
[13]Collect from the Mass for the Sixteenth Sunday after Pentecost.

I want you to learn perfect self-abnegation, and to live according to My will, without any grumbling or words of complaint coming from you.

Follow Me![1] *I am the Way, the Truth, and the Life.*[2] Without the Way, there is no going; without the Truth, there is no knowing; without Life, there is no living. I am the Way you are to follow; I am the Truth you are to believe; I am the Life you are to hope for.

I am the Way inviolable, the Truth infallible, and the Life illimitable.

I am the Way that is most straight, the Truth that is supreme, the Life that is true, blessed, and uncreated.

2. If you continue in My way *you will get to know the truth and the truth will set you free,*[3] and you will have eternal life.

If you wish to enter life, keep My commandments.[4]

If you wish to know the truth, believe in Me.

If you wish to be perfect, sell everything.[5]

If you wish to be My disciple, deny yourself.[6]

If you wish to enjoy a life of blessedness, despise this present life.

If you wish to be exalted in heaven, *humble yourself*[7] in this world.

If you wish to reign with Me, carry My cross. For only the servants of the cross will discover the way leading to beatitude and to true light.

Disciple:

3. Lord Jesus, since Your life was somewhat short and was despised by those in the world, grant that I may imitate You in

[1]Matt. 9:9 [2]John 14:6 [3]John 8:32 [4]Matt. 19:17
[5]Matt. 19:21 [6]Matt. 16:24 [7]Matt. 23:12

suffering the world's contempt. *The servant is not to be greater than his master, nor the disciple greater than his teacher.*[8]

Let Your servant seriously reflect on Your life, for there I find my salvation and genuine holiness. Whatever else I may read or hear, it neither refreshes me nor does it give me full delight.

Jesus:

4. My son, since you know these things and have read about them all, *blessed will you be if you practice them.*[9] *He who has My commandments and keeps them is the one who loves Me; I will love him and I will reveal Myself to him,*[10] and *I will have him sit with Me in My Father's kingdom.*[11]

Disciple:

Lord Jesus, let it be done as You have said and promised, and may I enjoy the fulfillment of that promise.

I have received the cross, yes, I have accepted it from Your hands. You have placed it upon me and I will support and sustain it until I die. The life of a good monk is indeed a cross, but it is also his guide to paradise. Now that we are on our way, we must not go backward nor abandon our purpose.

5. My brothers, take courage, and let us go forward together. Jesus will be with us. We have accepted the cross for Jesus' sake, and for Jesus' sake we will persevere in carrying it to the end.

He who is our Commander has gone before us and will be our helper. Look, our King marches ahead of us and will fight for us. Let us follow Him like men and not yield to fear. Let us

[8]Matt. 10:24 [9]John 13:17 [10]John 14:21
[11]Rev. 3:21

be prepared to die bravely in battle and not stain our glory by deserting the cross.[12]

57. *When You Commit Some Fault Do Not Yield to Depression*

Jesus:

My son, your patience and humility in time of adversity are more pleasing to Me than your great consolations and devotion during times of prosperity. Why do you give in to sadness when something slight is said against you? Even if something worse had been said, still you should not become disturbed.

But let it pass for now. This is not the first time this has happened to you, nor is it anything new. And if you have a long life ahead of you it won't be the last.

So long as no misfortune comes your way you are sufficiently brave; you give good advice to others and know the right words to use in encouraging them. But when some sudden and unexpected trial comes knocking on your own door, that advice and encouragement abandon you.

Keep in mind how frightfully weak you are when a troublesome trifle besets you, but remember, when this or a similar situation befalls you, it is all for your salvation.

2. Keep each trial outside your heart, as best you can, and if it has already knocked you down, don't let it keep you down nor keep you long under its power. If you cannot bear it cheerfully, at least bear it patiently.

Even if you are unwilling to bear the remark and feel anger

[12]Cf. 1 Macc. 9:10

rising in you, hold yourself in check and let no unbecoming word escape your lips that might give scandal to little ones. The inflamed emotion will soon calm down and the return of grace will change your inward sorrow into something sweet.

As I the Lord live, I am ready to help you and comfort you more than ever before; all you need do is put your trust in Me and devoutly call upon me.

3. Take courage, and gird yourself to endure still greater trials. Though you often see yourself harassed and severely tempted, still all is not lost. You are a man and not God; you are flesh and not an angel! How can you always persevere in the same state of virtue when even Lucifer failed the test in heaven and Adam did the same in paradise?

I am He who raises and rescues those who mourn, and those who readily acknowledge their weakness I lift up to have a share in My divinity.

Disciple:

4. Lord, blessed be Your word, *sweeter to my mouth than honey and the honeycomb.*[1] What would I do in my many trials and tribulations if You did not comfort me with Your holy words? Does it matter which and how many trials I undergo if in the end I arrive at heaven's harbor?

Grant me a good end and a pleasing passage out of this world. My God, remember me and direct me along the right road leading to Your kingdom. Amen.

[1]Ps. 119:103

58. Not Delving into Sublime Matters Nor into God's Secret Judgments

Jesus:

My son, take care not to discuss lofty topics and God's secret judgments, for example, why one individual is raised to higher graces while another is totally neglected; or why one is so highly exalted and another sorely afflicted. All this is beyond the power of human understanding, and no amount of reasoning or discussion can possibly fathom divine judgments.

Therefore, when the enemy suggests such things to you, or when some inquisitive man curiously asks you about them, answer in the words of the Prophet: *You are righteous, Lord, and Your judgments are right.*[1] Or in this way: *The Lord's judgments are true and justified in themselves.*[2] My judgments are to be respected and not discussed for they are incomprehensible to the human mind.[3]

2. And do not inquire into nor discuss the merits of the saints, disputing which one is the holier or which one the greater in the kingdom of heaven. Such questions, as a rule, engender useless quarrels and controversies; they likewise promote pride and presumption which, in turn, give rise to envy and dissension, all because one man arrogantly prefers one saint while another boastfully favors someone else.

Desiring to know and to delve into such matters is totally fruitless and is very displeasing to the saints themselves. *I am not the God of dissension but of peace,*[4] a peace founded more in true humility than in the exaltation of one's self.

3. Some individuals, in accord with their personal piety, are drawn to one or another of the saints, but this is a human

[1] Ps. 119:137 [2] Ps. 19:9 [3] Cf. Rom. 11:33
[4] 1 Cor. 14:33

affection or preference on their part and does not come from Me.

I am He who made all the saints; I gave them grace and I clothed them in glory.

I know each one's merits and *I went to meet them with the blessings of My sweetness.*[5]

I foreknew My beloved ones before all ages;[6] *I chose them from the world, they did not first choose Me.*[7]

I called them by grace;[8] I attracted them by mercy and I led them safely through many temptations.

I poured unheared of consolation into their hearts; I gave them the gift of perseverance and I crowned their patience.

4. I know who is first and who is last and I embrace each of them with an unspeakable love.

I am to be praised in My saints, and above all things I am to be blessed and honored in each of them whom I have so gloriously exalted and predestined without any regard for their merits.

Therefore, *he who slights one of the least of My saints*[9] shows no honor to the greatest because I have made both the small and the great. He who belittles one of My saints, belittles Me and all who live in the kingdom of heaven. There, all are one by the bond of love; everyone thinks the same thoughts and has the same desires and all love one another.

5. But what is still greater and more wonderful is this: they all love Me more than themselves and their own merits. Having been raised far above themselves and having been drawn from all self-love, they now live only to love Me in whom they find their rest and enjoy love's fruition. Nothing can now turn them from Me nor dishearten them for they are

[5]Ps. 21:3 [6]Cf. Rom. 8:29 [7]John 15:16, 19
[8]Gal. 1:15 [9]Matt. 18:10

filled with eternal Truth and burn with the inextinguishable fire of charity.

Let carnal and unspiritual men, therefore, be silent and not discuss the relative status of the saints, for the only love that these men know is self-love and self-gratification. They add to or subtract from the saints' glory according to their likes and dislikes, and not according to what pleases eternal Truth.

6. In many cases this is a question of pure ignorance, but especially in those who, because they are insufficiently enlightened from above, rarely know how to love anyone with a perfect spiritual love. Such individuals are drawn to one or another person by natural affection or human friendship, and because they are accustomed to so act on earth they think they can do the same with the saints in heaven.

There is an infinite gap beween the thoughts of the imperfect man and the thoughts of the enlightened man who has received them by heavenly revelation.

7. Therefore, My son, beware of becoming curious about matters that far exceed your powers of comprehension, rather make it your concern and pursuit to be included, even though you be the least, among those in the kingdom of God.

And if anyone were to know which saint is the holier in the kingdom of heaven or which one the greater, such knowledge would do him no good unless, acting upon it, he humbled himself before me and then rose to give greater praise to My name.

The man who argues about who is the greater or the lesser among the saints is much less acceptable to God than the man who reflects on the greatness of his sins, who realizes how little he has advanced in virtue, and sees how far he is from the perfection of the saints. It is better to invoke the saints with devout prayer and tears and humbly to implore their aid than, out of sheer curiosity, to inquire idly into their secrets.

8. The saints are perfectly and fully contented in heaven; would that men knew how to reach that same contentment and abstain from their empty babbling. The saints find no glory in their own merits and ascribe no goodness to themselves but all to Me, since it was I who gave them everything out of My abundant love. They are filled with so great a love of God and have such an overflowing joy that there is nothing lacking to their glory and nothing wanting to their happiness.

The higher the saints are in glory, the more humble they are in themselves, the closer they are to Me, and the more beloved by Me. You have it thus written: *They cast down their crowns before God and fell on their faces before the Lamb; and they adored Him who lives for ever and ever.*[10]

Many people do ask *who is the greatest in the kingdom of God,*[11] but they can't answer whether they themselves will one day be worthy to be numbered among the least in heaven.

9. It is a great grace to be even the least in heaven where everyone is great; every one of them *shall be called and shall be the children of God.*[12] *The least will be valued as a thousand, and the sinner, a hundred years old, will see death.*[13]

When the disciples asked who was the greatest in the kingdom of heaven, they received this response: *Unless you turn yourselves around and become like children, you will never enter the kingdom of heaven. Therefore, he who humbles himself like this child is the greatest in the kingdom of heaven.*[14]

10. Woe to those who refuse to humble themselves as children! The lowly gate to the heavenly kingdom will not permit them to enter. *Woe also to the rich who here have their consolations,*[15] for while the poor enter into God's kingdom the

[10]Rev. 4:10 [11]Matt. 18:1 [12]1 John 3:1 [13]Is. 60:22, 65:20
[14]Matt. 18:3-4

rich will stand outside lamenting their lot.

Rejoice, you humble! *Exult you poor because yours is the kingdom of God,*[16] that is, *if you walk in the way of the truth.*[17]

59. *Putting All Our Hope and Trust in God*

Disciple:

Lord, what can I rely on in this life? Or, of all the things under heaven's vault, which object is my greatest comfort? Is it not You, my Lord God, whose mercies are without number?

When You were absent from me, Lord, when did things go well? And how could they ever go amiss when You are with me? I would rather be poor for Your sake than be rich without You. I would rather be a pilgrim traveling the earth with You than be in heaven without You. Where You are there is heaven, and where You are not there is death and hell.

You are my sole desire and therefore I long for You, cry out to You and beseech You. There is no one in whom I can fully confide; there is no one whom I can trust to help me when in need, except You, my God. You are my hope and my trust; You console me and You are faithful in everything.

2. *Everybody looks after their own interests,*[1] but You look after my happiness and my salvation, and You see that all things work unto my good. Even though You send me various trials and temptations, You, who are accustomed to try Your beloved servants in a thousand different ways, design all this for my benefit, and I am to love and praise You no less during

[15]Luke 6:24 [16]Luke 6:20 [17]3 John 4
[1]Phil. 2:21

times of trial than I am when You fill me with consolation from heaven.

3. Therefore, it is in You, Lord God, that I put all my hope and trust; on You I lay all my anxieties and worries. Everything that is not You I find terribly unsteady and insecure.

My many friends are of no help to me, nor can influential associates aid me. Wise counselors can't offer me the correct answer, nor can the books of the learned give me any comfort. No precious stone can buy me my freedom, nor can any secret and tranquil place give me safety. None of these are any good to me unless You Yourself, Lord, assist and help me, comfort and console me, teach and defend me.

4. Whatever may seem good for our peace and happiness is really nothing if You are absent from us; of themselves all these things can do nothing for us.

You are the end of everything good, the highest point of life and the depth of wisdom. Your servant's greatest comfort is to place his trust in You above all else. *To You I raise my eyes.*[2] In You I trust, my God, the Father of mercies.[3]

Bless and sanctify my soul with Your heavenly blessing and let it become Your holy dwelling and the throne of Your eternal glory. Let nothing be found in Your respected temple that may offend the eyes of Your majesty.

According to the greatness of Your goodness and *the multitude of Your mercies, look upon me*[4] and hear my request, the prayer of Your poor servant, who sojourns here in distant exile in a region of shadows and death.

Guard and defend my soul living amid the many dangers of this corruptible life and by Your grace direct me along the paths of peace to my fatherland, the place of everlasting brightness. Amen.

[2]Ps. 123:1 [3]2 Cor. 1:3 [4]Ps. 69:16

BOOK IV
On the Blessed Sacrament

A Devout Exhortation To Receive Holy Communion

The Voice of Christ

Come to Me, all you who labor and are burdened and I will refresh you.[1] *The bread that I will give for the life of the world is My flesh.*[2]

Take and eat, this is My body, which is being given for you. Do this in memory of Me.[3] *He who eats My flesh and drinks My blood abides in Me and I abide in him.*[4] *These words that I have addressed to you are spirit and life.*[5]

[1]Matt. 11:28 [2]John 6:51 [3]Matt. 26:26; 1 Cor. 11:24
[4]John 6:56 [5]John 6:63

1. *The Reverence with Which Christ Should Be Received*

Disciple:

Christ, eternal Truth, You have spoken these words, though they were not all spoken at the same time, nor all recorded in the same place. But since they are Yours and are true, I receive them in faith and thanksgiving.

These are Your words and You have spoken them; they are also mine since You have uttered them for my salvation. I gladly accept them from Your lips and I want them deeply imprinted on my heart.

Your words are filled with compassion, sweetness, and love, and they encourage me, but my sins frighten me and my sullied conscience keeps me from receiving this great mystery. Though Your sweet and gentle words draw me, still the great number of my wrongdoings holds me back.

2. You command me to come to You in full confidence if I want *to have part in You,*[1] and to receive the food of immortality if I desire to attain eternal life and glory.

You say: *Come to Me, all you who labor and are burdened and I will refresh you.*[2] O how sweet and cordial are these words to the sinner's ear by which You, my Lord God, invite me, poor and needy as I am, to Communion in Your most holy Body. But, who am I, Lord, that I should be so bold as to approach

[1]John 13:8 [2]Matt. 11:28

You? Behold, *the heaven of heavens cannot contain You,*[3] and yet You say: *Come to Me, all of you.*

3. What means this kind deference, this friendly invitation? How can I dare come to You, since I know of nothing good in me on which I can rely? How can I bring You into my home, I who have so often done evil before Your loving eyes?

The angels and archangels adore You, the saints and the just in heaven reverence You, and still you say: *Come to Me, all of you.* If You Yourself had not said this, no one would have thought it true! If You had not commanded it, who would dare to approach You?

Behold, *Noah, that just man,*[4] labored a hundred years in building the ark so that he and a few others could be saved.[5] How then can I prepare myself in an hour to receive with due reverence the Creator of the world?

4. Moses, that great servant and special friend of Yours, built an Ark of incorruptible wood and overlaid it with the purest of gold[6] in order to house the Tablets of the Law, and how shall I, a corruptible creature, dare so easily to receive the Maker of the Law and the Giver of life?

Solomon, Israel's wisest king, *spent seven years in building that magnificent temple*[7] to Your name's honor and glory. *For eight days he celebrated the feast of its dedication*[8] and sacrificed a thousand peace offerings,[9] and amid the blare of trumpets solemnly and joyously brought the Ark of the Covenant to the place prepared for it. And I, poorest and most wretched of

[3] 1 Kings 8:27 [4] Gen. 6:9 [5] Cf. 1 Pet. 3:20
[6] Cf. Ex. 25:10-11 [7] 1 Kings 6:38 [8] 2 Macc. 2:12
[9] Solomon offered 1,000 offerings at Gibeon (1 Kings 3:4), but at the time of the dedication of the temple he offered 22,000 oxen and 120,000 sheep (1 Kings 8:63).

men, how shall I bring You into my home, who scarcely know how to spend a half-hour in devout prayer? Would that I were able to spend a single half-hour as I ought!

5. My God, how zealously these holy men tried to please You! But, alas, how little I accomplish! How short is the time I set aside for preparing myself for Communion! Rarely am I fully recollected, and still more rarely am I entirely free of distractions. When I am in Your saving presence, certainly, no improper thought should enter my mind, nor should a single thought of mine be focused on a creature. It is not an angel that I am about to receive as my guest, but the very lord of angels.

6. There is a vast difference between the Ark of the Covenant with the holy objects it contained, and Your most pure Body and its indescribable powers. There is an immense difference between the sacrifices of the Old Law that were a prefigurement of the one that was to come, and the true sacrifice of Your Body which completes those of ancient times.

Why, then, is my heart not aflame in Your holy presence? Why don't I more carefully prepare myself to receive You, when those holy and ancient patriarchs, prophets, kings and princes, and all the people manifested so great a devotion and love in worshipping You?

7. The devout and holy *King David danced before the Ark of God with all his might,*[10] recalling the blessings granted his ancestors. *He invented a variety of instruments,*[11] composed the Psalms, taught the people how to sing with glad hearts, and under the inspiration of the Holy Spirit frequently accompanied them on the harp. He taught the people of Israel to praise God with all their being and with one voice to proclaim and bless Him each day of their lives.

[10]2 Sam. 6:14 [11]Amos 6:5

If the devotion and praise of God manifested by these people in the presence of the Ark of the Covenant was so great, then how great should be the reverence that I, and every Christian, should have in the presence of this Holy Sacrament when we receive the most excellent Body of Christ?

8. Many people travel to different places to pay homage to the relics of the saints, and they stand in amazement when they see the splendid shrines, and are in awe when they hear narrated the story of the saints' lives and their remarkable deeds, or again, when they kiss the bones wrapped in silk and encased in gold. But, You, my God, the Holy of Holies, the Creator of all things and lord of angels, are here present before me on this altar!

It frequently happens that it was mere curiosity and a desire to see new things and new places that led these pilgrims to take to the road, and rarely does one hear about them amending their lives as a result of a trip that was spent mostly in exchanging gossip and with no thought of contrition for sins.

But, in the Sacrament of the altar, You, my God, the man Christ Jesus, are fully present, and as often as we worthily and devoutly receive You, we enjoy the abundant fruits of eternal salvation.

It is not frivolousness on our part, nor curiosity, nor a desire to delight the senses, that draws us to You, rather it is firm faith, holy hope, and a living love.

9. O veiled Creator of the world, how marvelously You treat us; how gently and graciously You favor Your elect, offering Yourself to them to be received in this Blessed Sacrament. This surpasses all understanding! You draw

devout hearts toward You and You set their love aflame for You.

And Your faithful ones, those who have devoted their whole life to seeking to amend their ways, often receive, in this most worthy Sacrament, the grace of devotion and love of virtue.

10. O admirable and hidden grace of the Sacrament, you are known only to Christ's faithful followers! Those who lack faith and are slaves of sin are incapable of recognizing this grace and sharing in it.

In this Sacrament spiritual grace is conferred, the soul's lost strength is replenished and its beauty, once disfigured by sin, is restored. And sometimes this grace, flowing from the fullness of devotion, not only fortifies the recipient's mind, but also gives strength to the body debilitated by sin.

11. Great should be our sorrow and regret because of our negligence and coolness in not being more fervently drawn to receive Christ, who is our only hope of salvation and our sole reward. He Himself is our sanctification and our redemption. It is He who consoles us in our daily pilgrimage and it is He who is the eternal happiness of the saints.

It is most sad to note that many people have little interest in this saving mystery that gives joy to heaven and keeps the whole world in being. How blind they are, and how hard their hearts, for not cherishing this most wonderful gift and for allowing themselves, because of frequent reception, to grow indifferent toward this Holy Sacrament.

12. If in the entire world this most Holy Sacrament were celebrated in only one place and consecrated by only one priest, how great do you think would be the desire impelling

men to travel to that one place and to be with that one priest of God so that they could be present at the celebration of the divine mysteries? But now there are many priests and Christ is offered in many places, and the more widespread through the world is this Holy Communion, the greater is the proof of God's grace and love for mankind.

Good Jesus, eternal Shepherd, I offer You my thanks for choosing to nourish us poor exiles with Your precious Body and Blood, and for inviting us, with Your own lips, to share in this mystery: *Come to Me, all you who labor and are burdened and I will refresh you.*[12]

2. *God's Great Goodness and Charity Are Manifest in This Sacrament*

Disciple:

Lord, trusting in Your great goodness and mercy, I come to You as one sick to his Savior, as one hungry and thirsty to the Fount of life, as a beggar to the King of heaven, as a servant to his Lord, as a creature to his Creator, as one sorrowing to his compassionate Counselor.

Why this favor that You should come to me?[1] Who am I that You should give Yourself to me? Does a sinner dare to appear before You? How is it that You deign to come to a sinner? You know your servant and You know there is no good in him whatever, so why show him this favor?

Indeed, I openly confess my worthlessness and I acknowledge Your goodness. I praise Your mercy and I thank You for Your great charity. It is Your goodness that leads You to do

[12]Matt. 11:28

[1]Luke 1:43

this and not any merits of mine. You do this so that Your goodness may be made more evident to me, that Your great charity be better revealed to me, and that Your humility be better recommended to me. Because this is what pleases You, You have commanded it to be; I appreciate Your bending toward me and I ask that my wickedness not turn You away from me.

2. O most sweet and gentle Jesus, what reverence, thanksgiving, and praise unending I owe You when I receive Your sacred Body. There is no man on earth who can adequately extol the excellence of this Sacrament. What thoughts should be mine when I approach You, my Lord, in Holy Communion? I can never honor You as You deserve, nevertheless, I am filled with the longing to receive You.

What better thought could I have, or what thought could be more profitable to me and helpful toward salvation than the full humbling of myself before You and praising Your infinite goodness toward me!

My God, I praise and magnify You without end; but myself I despise and in all my unworthiness I prostrate myself before You.

3. You are the Holy of Holies and I am the worst of sinners. You show Your favor to me who am unworthy to raise my face to You. You come to me; You desire to be with me and You invite me to Your banquet. You wish to give me heavenly food and *the bread of angels.*[2] You desire to give me Yourself, *the living bread that came down from heaven and gives life to the world.*[3]

4. O, whence this love, this resplendent graciousness toward me? How boundless should my gratitude and praise be to You for this gift of Yours!

[2]Ps. 78:25 [3]John 6:33, 51

O, how beneficial and salutary was Your decision to institute this Sacrament! How sweet and joyful the banquet in which You gave Yourself as food!

O, how admirable are Your works, Lord, how extraordinary Your power, and how unerring Your truth! You spoke and all things were made; this too was done as You had commanded it.

5. It is a wondrous mystery, one worthy of our faith and surpassing all human understanding, that You, my Lord God, true God and true man, are entirely present under the appearance of a little bread and wine[4] and that You are eaten by those who receive You but, still, You are not consumed.[5]

Lord of all things, and who have need of nothing[6] You chose to live among us by means of this Holy Sacrament; keep my heart and body undefiled that with a pure and peaceful conscience, I may more frequently celebrate and receive these mysteries which You have ordained for Your special honor and instituted as Your everlasting memorial.

6. Rejoice and give thanks, my soul, to God for leaving so noble a gift and so singular a comfort with us in this valley of tears. As often as you re-enact this mystery and receive Christ's Body, so often do you carry on the work of your redemption[7] and are made a sharer in the merits of Christ. Christ's charity is never diminished, and the magnitude of His atonement can never be exhausted!

You must, therefore, prepare yourself to receive this Blessed Sacrament with a totally different outlook, seriously reflecting

[4]Cf. Matins, Lesson 5, Feast of Corpus Christi. This Office is popularly attributed to St. Thomas Aquinas (c. 1225-1274).

[5]Cf. the sequence, *Laud, O Zion,* from the Mass for the Feast of Corpus Christi.

[6]2 Macc. 14:35

[7]Cf. Secret in Mass for Ninth Sunday after Pentecost.

on this great mystery of salvation. Whenever you celebrate Mass or participate in it, it ought to be as great to you, as new, and as consoling, as if that same day Christ had first descended into the Virgin's womb and become man, or again, as if He were hanging on the cross suffering and dying for the salvation of mankind.

3. *Benefits Coming from Frequent Communion*

Disciple:

I come to You, Lord, so that Your gift may benefit me and that I may be filled with the joy of Your holy banquet *which You, O God, in Your sweetness, have prepared for Your poor ones.*[1]

In You is all that I can and should desire. You are my salvation and my redemption, my hope and my strength, my honor and my glory. Therefore, *give joy this day to the soul of Your servant for to You, Lord Jesus, I lift up my soul.*[2]

I desire to receive You with devotion and reverence; I want to invite You into my house, and like Zacchaeus[3] I want to be worthy of Your blessing and be numbered among the children of Abraham. My soul longs to receive Your Body and my heart desires to be united to You.

2. Give Yourself to me and that is enough, apart from You there is nothing that can give me comfort. Without You I cannot exist, and without Your visits I am unable to live. I must, therefore, come to You often and receive You as the medicine of salvation, otherwise, deprived of this heavenly food, I shall faint on the way.

Most merciful Jesus, while preaching to the people and

[1]Ps. 68:10 [2]Ps. 86:4 [3]Cf. Luke 19:1-10

healing their many diseases, You once said: *I am unwilling to send them home fasting, lest they faint on the way.*[4] Treat me in the same way for You have left Yourself present in this Sacrament to be a comfort to Your faithful ones. You are the sweet refreshment of our souls and whoever eats You worthily shall be a partaker and heir of eternal glory.

Because I so often fall and commit sin, and because I so quickly grow lukewarm and am neglectful, it is most necessary that by frequent prayer, confession, and the devout reception of Your Body, I be renewed, cleansed, and have my soul enkindled lest, perhaps, by abstaining from Your Body for too long a time, I fall away from my holy resolve.

3. Because of man's senses, *he is prone to evil ever since his youth,*[5] and unless the divine medicine be administered to him, he will quickly fall into greater sins. Holy Communion, on the other hand, pulls him away from evil and strengthens him in goodness.

How lazy and lukewarm I am when I celebrate Mass or go to Holy Communion! What would it be like if I never had this remedy or if I never sought so great an aid! Though I may not have the proper dispositions, and thus be fully fit to celebrate Mass daily, still, I will strive to receive these divine mysteries at the appointed times and offer myself to share in so great a grace.

The faithful soul's chief comfort, while *away from You and still pilgrimaging in this mortal body,*[6] is to remember You and to receive You, the soul's Beloved, with great devotion.

4. O, Lord God, how wonderful is Your tender mercy toward us. Creator, who gives life to every spirit, deign to come to my poor undeserving soul and satisfy my hunger with

[4]Matt. 15:32 [5]Gen. 8:21 [6]2 Cor. 5:6

the fullness of Your humanity and divinity.

O happy mind and blessed soul, that deserves to receive You, its Lord God, with devotion, and in receiving You becomes filled with spiritual joy.

O how great a Lord she receives; how beloved a Guest she brings into her home; how sweet a Companion she welcomes; how faithful a Friend she greets; how comely and noble a Spouse she embraces, one whom she loves above all things and whom she desires above all things desirable.

O my sweet Beloved, let heaven, earth and everything beautiful in them be hushed in Your presence! Whatever loveliness and praiseworthiness they possess, they are all Your gifts. You have granted them out of your boundless generosity, and never will they attain the beauty of Your name, *whose wisdom is beyond all measure.*[7]

4. *Many Are the Benefits Bestowed on Those Who Receive Communion Devoutly*

Disciple:

My Lord God, give Your sweet blessing to Your servant that I may worthily and devoutly approach Your sublime Sacrament. Set my heart aflame with love for You and deliver me from my great apathy. Visit me with Your saving grace that I may spiritually savor Your kindness so admirably present in the Sacrament, as in its very source.[1]

Enlighten my eyes[2] that I may get a glimpse of this great

[7]Ps. 147:5

[1]Cf. Matins, Lesson 6, Feast of Corpus Christi [2]Ps. 13:3

mystery and strengthen me that I may believe it with a faith that knows no doubt. This is Your work and it is not within the power of man. This is Your holy institution and not any human invention.

There is no one capable of grasping and understanding this mystery by himself; it even transcends the subtle intelligence of the angels. How then can I, an unworthy sinner, only *ashes and dust,*[3] grasp and comprehend so lofty and holy a mystery?

2. Lord, *in the uprightness of my heart,*[4] and in accordance with Your command, I come to You, filled with honor, hope, and a sincere and secure faith; I truly believe that You, God and man, are here present in this Sacrament.

Since You want me to receive You and to be united to You in love, I beg Your mercy and I implore You to grant me this special grace, namely, that I may be dissolved and become one with You and be filled with Your love so that I may never again give thought to consolation coming from outside.

This most worthy and most revered Sacrament is the salvation of our soul and body and the medicine for every spiritual illness. In this Sacrament we have a cure for our wickedness and a curb to our passions. In addition, it conquers or reduces temptation, pours greater grace into our hearts, gives growth to virtue, fortifies our faith, strengthens our hope, and enkindles and expands our love.

3. My God, You, who are the Custodian of my soul, the Healer of all human weakness, and Giver of all interior consolation, have granted through this Sacrament many blessings to Your beloved ones who devoutly receive You in Holy Communion.

You pour much consolation into their hearts and thus You

[3]Sir. 17:32 [4]1 Chr. 29:17

support them in their many trials and raise them up from the depths of dejection to the hope of Your protection. Likewise, by a new grace You refresh and interiorly enlighten them so that they who felt some anxiety and were lacking in love before receiving Holy Communion, now find themselves greatly changed for the better, having been fed on the food and drink of heaven.

You treat Your chosen ones in this manner so that they may truly recognize and clearly experience their own weakness and acknowledge how much grace and goodness they receive from Your hands. Of themselves they are frigid, hard, and without devotion, but through You they become fervent, devout, and zealous.

Shall not the man who humbly approaches the fountain of sweetness carry back with him a cup of its sweet liquid? Shall not the man who stands next to a blazing fire enjoy some of its heat? You are the fountain, always abundant and overflowing; You are the ever-burning fire never to be quenched.[5]

4. If I cannot draw from the fullness of this fountain, nor drink until my thirst is fully slaked, I will then put my lips to the spout of that heavenly spring and receive at least a droplet to relieve my thirst and to keep me from withering away.

And if I cannot be wholly heavenly, and if I cannot be on fire like the Cherubim and Seraphim, I will, still, try to be devout and prepare my heart so as to gain some small spark of the divine fire by humbly receiving this life-giving Sacrament.

Good Jesus, most holy Savior, from Your boundless goodness supply me with all that I need, for You Yourself have invited everyone to come to You: *Come to Me all you who labor and are burdened and I will refresh you.*[6]

[5]Cf. Augustine, *Confessions* X, 29 [6]Matt. 11:28

5. Indeed, *I labor with the sweat of my brow,*[7] my heart is tormented with grief and I am crushed under the weight of sin. I am troubled with temptation, entangled and oppressed by many evil passions. There is no one to help me, no one to free me, no one to save me, but You, Lord God my Savior. To You I commit myself and all that I have, and I ask You to protect me and to lead me to eternal life.

You who have provided Your Body and Blood as my food and drink, receive me for the praise and glory of Your name. My God and my salvation, by the reception of Your most sacred mysteries, allow me to grow in devotion and in love of You.[8]

5. *The Dignity of the Blessed Sacrament and of the Priesthood*

Jesus:

If you had the purity of the angels and the holiness of St. John the Baptist, you would still not be worthy to receive or touch the Blessed Sacrament. It is not because of any merits on man's part that man consecrates and handles Christ's Sacrament and *eats the bread of angels.*[1]

Noble is the ministry of the priest and exalted his dignity. To him has been granted what has not been granted to the angels. Only a priest, duly ordained in the Church, has the power to celebrate Mass and consecrate the Body of Christ. The priest is God's instrument and by God's institution and

[7]Gen. 3:19

[8]Cf. Postcommunion, in the Mass for the Fourth Sunday of Advent

[1]Ps. 78:25

command he speaks God's word, but God always remains the chief author and the invisible worker, to whom all things are subject and to whose command everything is obedient.

2. With reference to what pertains to this most excellent Sacrament you ought to believe Almighty God more than your own thinking or any visible sign. Therefore, you should approach this Sacrament with reverent awe.

Take a look at yourself[2] and consider the office *entrusted to you through the imposition of the bishop's hands.*[3] You were made a priest and were consecrated to celebrate Mass. See that you faithfully, devoutly and at the appointed time offer this sacrifice to God and see that *your life is above reproach.*[4]

By becoming a priest you have not diminished your burden, but have taken on a stricter discipline, and are now obliged to strive for greater perfection and holiness. A priest should be adorned with every virtue, and be *a model of good deeds to others.*[5] His time should be spent not as the common man spends his, but *with the angels in heaven,*[6] or with men who are considered perfect on earth.

3. When clad in sacred vestments the priest takes the place of Christ and humbly and suppliantly intercedes before God *for himself and for all people.*[7] On his vestments he wears the sign of the cross, in front as well as behind him, to keep Christ's passion always in mind. He wears a cross on the front of his chasuble that he may carefully observe Christ's footsteps and fervently strive to follow them.[8] And he is marked with a cross on the back that he may cheerfully suffer for God's sake all the trials that others may choose to impose upon him.

[2]1 Tim. 4:16 [3]1 Tim. 4:14 [4]1 Tim. 3:2 [5]Tit. 2:7
[6]Phil. 3:20 [7]Heb. 5:3 [8]Cf. 1 Pet. 2:21

The priest wears the cross in front to mourn his own wrongdoings, and behind him to lament, with compassion, the sins of others, all the time remembering that he has been appointed mediator between God and sinners. The priest must not grow weary of prayer nor of offering the Holy Sacrifice until the time comes for God to grant His mercy and grace.

When a priest offers Mass he gives honor to God, grants joy to the angels, builds up the Church, helps the living, obtains rest for the dead, and himself becomes a partaker in all good things.

6. *Preparation for Communion*

Disciple:

Lord, when I reflect on Your great dignity and my utter worthlessness, I tremble all over and I cover my face in shame. If I do not approach Your Sacrament, I flee life; if I receive it unworthily, I then incur Your displeasure. My God, my helper, my counselor in my every need, what am I to do?

2. Teach me the right way and give me some short exercise suitable for receiving Holy Communion. I would like to know how I can fervently and devoutly prepare myself to receive Your most salutary Sacrament, or to celebrate so great and sacred a Sacrifice.

7. *An Examination of Conscience and the Purpose of Amendment*

Jesus:

It is especially with a heart full of humility, meekness, and reverence, together with complete faith and firm intention of honoring God, that God's priest should approach the altar to celebrate Mass or to administer or receive this Sacrament.

Examine your conscience with great care, and cleanse and purify it as best you can by true contrition and a humble confession. Thus, nothing grievous will remain in you and you will know of nothing that could cause you remorse and hinder your free access to Me.

In general, be sorry for all your sins, but in particular, you must grieve and bewail those offenses you commit every day. If time then allows, speak to God in the secret mansions of your heart about the miseries your passions cause you.

2. Be sorry for the following: that you are so carnal and worldly, that your passions are still unmortified, and that you are so filled with evil desires;

so unguarded in your external senses and so frequently occupied with foolish fantasies;

so interested in worldly affairs and so indifferent about the interior life;

so quick for laughter and dissipation, but so averse to tears and sorrow;

so ready for relaxation and bodily comfort, but so sluggish to practice penance and devotion;

so eager to hear the latest news and to visit interesting places, but so slow in embracing what is humble and poor;

so desirous to have many possessions, but so miserly in giving and so tenacious in retaining;

so inconsiderate in your speech and so reluctant to observe silence;

so undisciplined in behavior and so rash in conduct;

so avid about food, but so deaf to God's word;

so prompt for rest, but so tardy for work;

so awake to listen to stories, but so sleepy for night vigils;

so hasty to end your prayers and so taken up with day-dreams;

so negligent in reciting the Office, so lukewarm in celebrating Mass, and so lacking in devotion in receiving Holy Communion;

so swiftly distracted and so rarely recollected;

so suddenly brought to anger and so easy to take offense;

so rapid to judge others and so severe in rebuke;

so happy in prosperity and so depressed in adversity;

so willing to make good resolves, but so unwilling to keep them.

3. After you have confessed and expressed your contrition for these and your other sins, and being dissatisfied with your own weakness, make a firm purpose to amend your ways and to make better progress in virtue.

Then, by the total resignation of your will, offer yourself on the altar of your heart as a perpetual holocaust in honor of My name. Faithfully entrust your body and soul to Me and thus you will be worthy to approach the altar to offer sacrifice to God and to receive the Sacrament of My Body unto your salvation.

4. There is no offering more worthy, nor any sacrifice more efficacious for the washing away of sins than for a man to offer

himself, purely and entirely, to God at the time that he offers My Body in the Mass or in Communion.

If a man does his best and is truly penitent, then whenever he approaches Me for grace and forgiveness, I will say: *As I live, I desire not the death of the sinner but that he turn from his ways and live.*[1] *His sins I will no longer remember and all shall be forgiven him.*[2]

8. *Christ's Offering on the Cross and the Resignation of Ourselves*

Jesus:

With My hands outstretched on the cross and My body naked, I willingly offered Myself to God the Father for your sins. Everything in Me was taken up in that sacrifice of divine propitiation. In like manner, you must willingly offer yourself to Me as a pure and holy oblation, with your whole heart and soul, and as lovingly as you can.

I ask nothing less of you but that you endeavor to resign yourself completely to Me. Whatever else you offer Me besides yourself does not interest me; *I do not seek your gift,*[1] what I seek is you.

2. If you possessed all things you would still not be satisfied unless you had Me, so whatever you offer Me doesn't please me if you yourself are not among your gifts. Offer yourself to Me and give your whole self to God, and your offering will be acceptable.

I gave My entire self to the Father for you and I gave My

[1]Ez. 33:11 [2]Is. 43:25 [1]Phil. 4:17

whole Body and Blood as food so that I could be totally yours and that you might be Mine forever. But if you hold yourself back and do not freely offer yourself to My will, then your offering will be incomplete and the union between us will not be perfect.

Therefore, if you want to receive grace and attain freedom, then a free oblation of yourself into God's hands must go before all your other offerings. This is why so few find enlightenment and interior freedom — they do not know how to renounce themselves completely.

This is My changeless teaching: *Unless you renounce all that you have, you cannot be my disciple.*[2] Therefore, if you desire to be My disciple, offer yourself to Me together with your whole heart.

9. *Offering Ourselves and All We Have to God and Praying for Others*

Disciple:

Lord, all that is contained in the heavens and on the earth is Yours.[1]

I desire, Lord, to give myself to You as a voluntary offering and to be Yours eternally. With a sincere heart I give myself to You this day, as Your servant forever, wishing to serve You in obedience and as a sacrifice of endless praise. Receive me together with this Holy Sacrifice of your precious Body, which today I offer You in the presence of Your unseen angels, attending You in heaven, that it may benefit my salvation and that of all Your people.

[2]Luke 14:33

[1]1 Chr. 29:11

2. Lord, on Your altar of sacrifice, I place before You all my sins and offenses which I have committed in Your sight and in that of Your holy angels, from the day that I was first able to sin up to this very hour. Set them all on fire by the flame of Your love and fully consume them; wash out the stains of my sins and *cleanse my conscience*[2] of all guilt; restore to me Your grace lost by my wrongdoing; grant me full pardon and graciously receive me back into Your friendship with a kiss of peace.

3. What can I do about my sins but make a humble confession of them, lament them, and beg Your forgiveness without end? Mercifully hear me, O my God, as I stand in Your presence and beseech You. My sins are especially loathsome to me; I never want to commit them again. I regret them and will regret them as long as I live, and I am prepared to do penance and make satisfaction for them as best I can.

Pardon me, O my God, *pardon my sins for the sake of Your holy name,*[3] and save my soul *which You have ransomed by Your precious Blood.*[4] I hand myself over to Your mercy and confidently place myself in Your hands. Deal with me *according to Your goodness and not as my sins and wickedness deserve.*[5]

4. I also offer You all my good deeds, though they be few in number and far from perfect. I ask You to make them better and sanctify them, make them pleasing and acceptable to You, and bring them to perfection. And in the end lead me, so lazy, useless, and puny a man, to a blessed and worthy end.

5. Likewise, I place before You all the holy desires the devout entertain in their hearts, the needs of my parents, friends, brothers and sisters, and of all who are dear to me; as well as the needs of those benefactors who, because of their

[2]Heb. 9:14 [3]Ps. 25:11 [4]1 Pet. 1:18, 19
[5]1 Macc. 13:46

love for You, have been generous to me and others. And also for the needs of those who have desired and requested me to offer Masses and prayers for themselves and their loved ones, who are still alive in the flesh or may have already departed this world. May all these experience the help of Your grace and the support of Your consolation; may they enjoy protection from all danger and freedom from all suffering, and being delivered from all such evils, may they joyfully return most splendid thanks to You.

6. I offer You, too, my prayers and this peace-bringing Sacrifice, for those especially who have in some way offended, grieved, or insulted me, or have caused me some loss or brought me some injury; and likewise for all whom I have at one time or another grieved, troubled, injured, or offended by my words, knowingly or unknowingly. I beg You to forgive these sins and offenses of ours committed against one another.

Lord, take from our hearts all suspicion, bitterness, anger, and quarrelsomeness, and all that can wound charity and lessen fraternal love. Have mercy, Lord, have mercy on those who seek Your mercy! Grant Your grace to those who need it, and make us live so as to be worthy to enjoy Your grace and may we make progress on our way to eternal life! Amen.

10. *Holy Communion Ought Not To Be Readily Deferred*

Jesus:

If you seek healing for your passions and habits, and desire to be made stronger and become more vigilant against the devil's deceits and temptations, then you must have frequent recourse to the fountain of grace and divine mercy, the fountain of goodness and all purity. Aware of the great fruit and healing power within the Sacrament, the enemy tries with all his might — in every way and at every opportunity — to hinder and prevent the faithful and devout person from receiving it.

2. Some people, while preparing themselves to receive Holy Communion, become the object of Satan's worst attacks. This wicked spirit, Job tells us, walks among the children of God[1] to molest them with his usual villainy, intimidating and so confusing them that he decreases their devotion. By unrelenting attack he weakens their faith with the result that they either give up going to Communion altogether or they receive it coldly and indifferently.

Pay no attention to the enemy's wiles or to the images he instills in your minds — no matter how horrid and shameful they be — but hurl all these phantasms back upon his head. That wretch is to be despised and treated with derision, and never should you omit going to Holy Communion because of his insulting remarks, or because of any disturbance he may stir up within you.

3. Some people refrain from going to Holy Communion because of an undue concern whether they are sufficiently devout, or because of some anxiety about going to confession. In this matter, follow the counsel of someone who is wise and banish all anxiety and scruple, for such thinking is a hindrance to God's grace and it destroys whatever devotion is in the soul.

Don't give up receiving Holy Communion because of some trivial matter or trifling annoyance, but quickly go and confess it, and gladly forgive all who have offended you. And if you

[1]Cf. Job 1:7

have offended anyone, then humbly ask God's pardon and He will generously forgive you.

4. What advantage is there in delaying confession or putting off Holy Communion? Cleanse yourself immediately; spit out the poison and be quick to take the antidote and you will feel much better than if you kept delaying for a long time. If, for some reason, you omit Communion today, a more serious reason may arise tomorrow and, thus, you can be kept from Communion for a long period, and each succeeding day you will feel more and more unfit to receive the Sacrament.

Rid yourself, and as speedily as you can, of your present sloth and sluggishness, for it does you no good whatever to live with such uneasiness and disquiet and to deprive yourself of the divine mysteries because of the snags you daily meet in life. In fact, you do yourself more harm by postponing Communion, for such delay usually results in still greater listlessness of soul.

Sad to say, some lazy and loose individuals eagerly look for reasons for putting off their confession, and consequently, they postpone their Communion; they know they would otherwise have to exert greater watchfulness over themselves.

5. O, how little the love and how weak the devotion of those who so readily defer receiving Holy Communion! But, how blessed and pleasing to God is the man who so lives and preserves his conscience in purity that every day he would be ready and prepared to receive Communion, if this were permitted and if he were able to do so without attracting too much attention.[2]

If someone abstains out of humility or for some reasonable

[2]The practice of frequent and even daily Communion only dates from Pope St. Pius X's decree in 1905.

cause, his reverence for the Sacrament should be commended. But if it is laziness that has taken hold of him, then he must rouse himself with all the strength he has, and God will indeed come to his aid for He looks with special favor on a man's good intention.

6. If a person, however, is legitimately prevented from receiving Communion and perseveres in his good will and holy desires, he will not be without the fruit that the Sacrament gives. Any and every devout individual, at any hour of any day, may with profit to his soul make a spiritual Communion with Christ, since there is nothing to prevent him from doing so. But on certain fixed days, and during certain seasons of the year, he ought with loving reverence receive the Body of his Redeemer sacramentally, and seek the praise and honor of God more than his own consolation.

As often as you receive this mystical Communion with Christ and are invisibly fed by Him, so often do you recall the mysteries of His Incarnation and Passion and become inflamed with love for Him.

7. The man who prepares himself only when some feast is approaching, or when the custom of the house prescribes, will most often find himself unprepared. Blessed is the man who, each time he celebrates Mass or receives Holy Communion, offers himself as a sacrifice to the Lord.

When celebrating Mass, don't take too long a time, nor be too hasty, but follow the practice common among those with whom you live. Don't be a source of weariness to others and don't make yourself a pest, but keep the custom of the house as established by our founders, and seek to serve others rather than following your own personal preferences and private devotions.

11. The Body of Christ and the Holy Scriptures Are Especially Necessary to the Faithful Soul

Disciple:

O sweet Lord Jesus, how great is the sweetness in that devout soul that feasts with You at Your banquet, where no other food is set before her but Yourself, her only Beloved, more desirable than all that the heart can desire.

It would indeed be sweet for me to shed tears in Your presence, tears coming from the depths of my love, and with the holy Magdalene bathe Your feet with them.[1] But, where is my devotion and where this cascade of holy tears?

In Your sight and in that of Your holy angels my whole heart should certainly be on fire and weep with joy, for here in this Sacrament You are truly present, though hidden beneath another form.[2]

2. If You were present here with all the brightness of Your divinity, my eyes could not bear to gaze upon You, nor could the whole world endure the splendor of the glory of your majesty. But by concealing Yourself beneath the Sacrament You have graciously taken my weakness into account. I truly have You here and I adore You whom the angels adore in heaven; I see You now through faith's veil but they see You as You really are.[3]

I must remain content with the light of true faith and walk in it *until the day when eternal light breaks through and shadowy forms pass away.*[4] But, *when that which is perfect does come,*[5] the need for Sacraments will cease for the blessed, who are in

[1]Cf. Luke 7:37-38

[2]Cf. Matins, Lesson 5, Feast of Corpus Christi [3]Cf. 2 Cor. 5:7

[4]Song 2:17 [5]1 Cor. 13:10

heavenly glory, will no longer have need of sacramental remedies. In God's presence the blessed find endless joy and behold His glory face to face, and now that they are *transformed from one degree of glory into the glory*[6] of the unfathomable Godhead, they taste the Word of God made flesh as He was in the beginning, and will remain forever.

3. When I think of these wonders I grow so weary with life and even spiritual consolation is boring. As long as I do not clearly see my Lord in all His glory, all that I do see and hear in this world means absolutely nothing to me.

O God, You are my witness;[7] nothing can console me, nor can any creature satisfy me, except You, my God, whom I desire to contemplate for ever and ever. But as long as I am in this mortal life, this is impossible to me and, hence, I must strive to acquire great patience and learn to submit myself and all my desires to You.

Your saints, Lord, now rejoicing with You in the kingdom of heaven, spent their lives in *faith and great patience,*[8] *awaiting the coming of Your glory.*[9] What the saints believed, I also believe; what they hoped for, I too hope for; and whither they have arrived, there I, trusting in Your grace, also hope to arrive.

In the meantime, *I will walk in faith,*[10] finding comfort in the examples of the saints. And *I will have the holy books to encourage me*[11] and be as a mirror of life. But, even above all these, Your most holy Body will be my singular remedy and special refuge.

4. Two things, I strongly feel, are most necessary to me in this life, and without them this life, with all its miseries, would be unbearable. Living as a captive prisoner in this body of

[6] 2 Cor. 3:18 [7] Rom. 1:9 [8] Heb. 6:12 [9] Tit. 2:13
[10] 2 Cor. 5:7 [11] 1 Macc. 12:9

mine, I acknowledge that I require two things, namely, food and light. Thus, you have granted me, in my weakness, Your sacred Body as the refreshment of both my soul and body, and You *have given me Your word as a lamp unto my feet.*[12] Without these two I cannot rightly live: the word of God is the light of my soul and Your Sacrament is the bread of life.

We can view these as two tables, placed on either side of the treasury of Holy Church. One table is the holy altar, with the holy bread, that is, Christ's precious Body; the other is the table of the divine law containing the holy doctrines that teach the right faith and unerringly lead us *through the inner veil into the Holy of Holies.*[13]

Lord Jesus, *Light of eternal light,*[14] I give You thanks for the table of sacred teaching, which You have provided for us through Your servants, the prophets, apostles, and other teachers.

5. Creator and Redeemer of all mankind, I thank You for having manifested Your love to the whole world by preparing a great supper in which You served not a lamb in type, but Your most sacred Body and Blood. By this sacred banquet You give joy to all the faithful and refresh them with the cup of salvation containing all the delights of paradise; the holy angels, likewise, feast with us, and their joy is even greater than ours.

6. O how great and honorable is the ministry of priests to whom it is given to consecrate with sacred words the Lord of majesty, to bless Him with their lips, to hold Him in their hands, to receive Him with their mouths, and to administer Him to others.

How clean those hands should be, how pure the mouth,

[12]Ps. 119:105 [13]Cf. Heb. 6:19 [14]Wis. 7:26

how holy the body, how sinless the heart of a priest, into whom the author of purity so frequently enters! Nothing should come from the mouth of a priest, who so often partakes of this Sacrament, but words that are holy, becoming, and edifying.

7. Since the priest's eyes are accustomed to look upon Christ's Body, they must be chaste and modest, and his hands, that touch the Creator of heaven and earth, must be pure and ever *lifted toward heaven.*[15] What is said in the Law is especially directed to priests: *Be holy, because I the Lord, your God, am holy.*[16]

8. Almighty God, let Your grace assist us, who have undertaken the priestly ministry, that we may serve You worthily, devoutly, and *with pure heart and good conscience.*[17] And if we cannot live in that degree of innocence of life as we ought, grant us, at least, to weep for the evil we have done, and in a spirit of humility and with a firm will for amendment, to serve You more fervently in the future.

12. *Receiving Christ in Holy Communion Demands Diligent Preparation*

Jesus:

I am the lover of purity and the giver of all holiness. I seek a pure heart and *it is there that I will make My rest.*[1] *Prepare a large furnished upper room*[2] for Me, and I will celebrate the Pasch with you and My disciples.

[15] 1 Tim. 2:8 [16] Lev. 19:2 [17] 1 Tim. 1:5
[1] Acts 7:49 [2] Mark 14:15

If you wish Me to come to you and remain with you, *throw away the old leaven*[3] and make clean the mansions of your heart. Shut out the whole world and all its sinful din and *sit as a solitary sparrow on a housetop*[4] and, *in the bitterness of your soul,*[5] meditate on your transgressions.

Every lover prepares the best and most beautiful room in the house for his beloved, and thus he shows his love for his invited friend.

2. You must realize that by yourself you cannot make proper preparations to receive Me, even if you spent a whole year trying and had nothing else to do! It is only through My kind graciousness that you are allowed to approach My table; as if a beggar had been invited to a rich man's dinner and had nothing to offer his host in return for his generosity, but to humble himself and express his thanks.

Do what you can, but do it with dedication, not out of habit or necessity; and with reverence and love receive the Body of your beloved Lord and God, who deigns to come to you. It is I who have invited you, and I who have ordered it to be so. I will supply what is wanting in you; come and receive Me!

3. When I bestow the grace of devotion on you, give thanks to your God, not because you deserve this grace but because I have been merciful toward you. But if you do not feel devout and find your soul quite dry, keep on praying, sighing to heaven, and knocking at My door.[6] Don't stop until you become worthy of receiving some crumb or drop of saving grace.

You need Me, I do not need you. You do not come to sanctify Me, but it is I who come to make you holier and

[3]1 Cor. 5:7 [4]Ps. 102:7 [5]Is. 38:15 [6]Cf. Matt. 7:7

better. You come to Me to be sanctified and to be united to Me, to receive new graces and to be inflamed once more with the desire to amend your life. *Don't neglect this grace,*[7] but prepare your heart with the greatest care and welcome your Beloved into your home.

4. You should not only make a devout preparation before receiving Holy Communion, but you should also carefully seek to preserve that grace after receiving the Sacrament. The same vigilance is necessary after receiving Communion as a devout preparation is necessary before. An alert watchfulness after Communion is the best way of preparing yourselves to receive even greater graces in the future. If, after Communion, we immediately busy ourselves in worldly affairs and seek outside consolation, then we only make ourselves more and more unfit for these graces.

Beware of too much talking. Remain in the quiet of your room and there enjoy your God, for you have Him whom the whole world cannot take from you.

I am He to whom you should offer your complete self, so that, freed from all anxious cares, you may live, no longer in yourself, but in Me.

13. *The Devout Soul Desires To Be United to Christ in the Blessed Sacrament*

Disciple:

Lord, how I would like to be alone with You, open my whole heart to You, and enjoy You as my soul desires; *let no one*

[7] 1 Tim. 4:14

despise me,[1] nor any creature disturb or concern me. I only want You to speak to me and I to You, as a beloved speaks to his beloved, or as a friend feasts with a friend.

This is my prayer and my desire: to be wholly united to You, to withdraw my heart from all created things, and to learn to savor heavenly and eternal realities by receiving Holy Communion or by frequently celebrating Mass.

O Lord God, when will I be totally united to You, completely absorbed in You and entirely forgetful of myself? *You in me and I in You!*[2] Grant that we may always remain united together.

2. Truly, You are *my Beloved, chosen from among thousands,*[3] in whom my soul is pleased to dwell all the days of my life.

Truly, You are the giver of peace, in whom there is supreme peace and true rest, and outside of whom there is only toil, sorrow, and endless misery.

Truly, *You are a hidden God,*[4] and have no dealings with the wicked, but have friendly converse with those who are humble and simple.

O how delightful, Lord, is Your Spirit, who, to manifest Your sweetness toward Your children, deigned to refresh them with the most sweet bread that came down from heaven.

Truly, there *is no other nation so great, that has its gods so near to it as You, our God, are near to all Your faithful,*[5] and for whose daily comfort You raise their hearts to heaven and give Yourself to them as their food and enjoyment.

3. For what people is as favored as the Christian people? Or what creature under heaven is so beloved as the devout soul into whom God enters and feeds with His glorious Body?

[1]Song 8:1 [2]John 17:21 [3]Song 5:10 [4]Is. 45:15
[5]Deut. 4:7

O unspeakable grace! O admirable condescension!

O boundless love, bestowed exclusively on man!

What return shall I make to the Lord[6] for this grace, for so exceptional a love? Nothing would be more pleasing than to offer my whole heart to God and unite myself intimately to Him. Indeed, everything within me shall rejoice when my soul shall be perfectly joined to Him.

Then God will say to me: "If you desire to be with Me, I desire to be with you." And in return I will answer Him: "Lord, be pleased to remain in me; most willingly do I wish to be with You."

This is my one and only desire, that my heart be united to You.

14. The Ardent Desire of Some Devout Persons To Receive the Body of Christ

Disciple:

How great and abundant is your greatness, Lord, which You have reserved for those who fear You![1] When I think of the many devout persons who, so piously and with such love in their hearts, approach Your Sacrament, Lord, my face reddens with shame realizing that I go to Your altar and the table of Holy Communion with a tepid and indifferent heart.

Why am I so dry and have so lukewarm a heart? Why am I not fully on fire when in Your presence, my God? Why am I not so powerfully attracted and enkindled as many of the devout are? They have such a fervent desire to receive Holy

[6]Ps. 116:12

[1]Ps. 31:19

Communion and their hearts so brim with love that they can not hold back their tears. Their souls and bodies *long for you, long from their very depths, O God,*[2] the fountain of life, and it is only by receiving Your Body with all delight and spiritual yearning that they can allay or satisfy their hunger.

2. How genuine their burning faith! A sure and convincing proof of Your sacred presence!

Indeed, the devout truly recognize their Lord in the breaking of the bread;[3] their hearts burning so strongly within because Jesus walks with them. But as for me, such affection and devotion, and so keen a love and desire are often far from me!

Good Jesus, sweet and gentle, have mercy on me and grant me, who am but a poor beggar, that when I receive Holy Communion I may sometimes experience just a touch of that heartfelt love for You. Thus, my faith in You will find strengthening, my hope in Your goodness will have its increase, and my love, set on fire by having tasted the heavenly manna, will never again grow faint.

3. Your mercy is powerful enough to grant me this most desired grace, and compassionate enough to bestow this spirit of fervor on me at a time when it suits Your divine pleasure.

Though I do not now burn with the same degree of longing as the very devout do, nevertheless, by Your grace, I desire to have that same intense craving as they have. I pray and earnestly desire to be numbered among Your devout lovers and to dwell in their holy company.

[2]Ps. 42:1-2 [3]Cf. Luke 24:30-35

15. *The Grace of Devotion Is Won by Humility and Self-Denial*

Jesus:

You must seek the grace of devotion with perseverance, ask for it with earnestness, await it with patient confidence, receive it with thankfulness, retain it with humility, and use it with great care. But, while you await its coming, entrust to God the time and manner of this heavenly gift.

When you feel little or no devotion within you, you should especially humble yourself, but not to the point of becoming excessively sad or overly dejected. God often grants in one brief moment what He has denied over a long period, and sometimes it is only at prayer's end that God grants what he delayed giving when it began.

2. If grace were always immediately granted, and were yours just for the asking, man's weakness would not be able to cope with it. The grace of devotion, therefore, must be awaited with solid hope and humble patience. And if the grace be not granted, or if it be mysteriously withdrawn, then charge it against yourself and your sins.

Sometimes it is but a trifling matter that keeps or hinders grace from coming to you, if indeed such a matter can be called trifling and not serious, since it prevents so much good from coming to you. But if you remove the obstacle, no matter how small or large it be, and fully overcome it, you will receive what you desire.

3. The sooner you resign yourself with your whole heart to God, and no longer seek anything according to your own will or pleasure, but totally place yourself in His hands, the sooner you will find that you are united to God and are at peace.

Nothing will make you happier or please you as much as being obedient to the divine will.

Therefore, whoever, with singleness of heart, raises his mind to God and empties himself of all unregulated attraction or aversion for creatures, he is the one who is fit to receive the gift of grace and worthy of the grace of devotion. The Lord grants His blessings there where He finds empty vessels.

The more perfectly a man renounces the things of earth and the more he dies to himself by practicing self-contempt, the more quickly does grace come to him, the more abundantly does it enter his soul, and the higher is his unencumbered soul raised upward.

4. At that moment, he shall see and feel himself enriched, he shall be filled with wonder and his heart shall expand within him,[1] for *the hand of the Lord is upon him*[2] because he has put himself totally into the Lord's hands forever.

Thus, the man *who seeks God with his whole heart is blessed,*[3] and does not possess his soul in vain. In receiving Holy Communion such a man obtains the great grace of divine union because he considers not his own personal devotion or consolation, but goes beyond all devotion and consolation and seeks only the glory and honor of God.

16. *Placing Our Needs before Christ and Asking His Grace*

Disciple:

O most sweet and most loving Lord, whom I now devoutly desire to receive, You know my weakness and what my needs

[1]Cf. Is. 60:5 [2]Acts 11:21 [3]Ps. 119:2

are. You know the evil habits and vices with which I struggle, and you know how frequently I feel troubled and tempted, and how disturbed and sullied my soul is. I come to You for healing, and I pray to You for comfort and relief.

I speak to one who knows all things, to whom all my inward thoughts and desires are clearly manifest, and who alone can help me and adequately console me. You know what good things I most need and You know how poor I am in practicing virtue.

2. Behold, poor and naked I stand before You, begging grace and imploring mercy. Feed this hungry beggar of Yours; inflame my coldness with the fires of Your love; enlighten my blindness with the brightness of your presence!

Change all worldly things into bitterness for me and change all that is onerous and adverse into patient forbearance. Make me despise and be ever forgetful of the base things of this earth.

Raise my heart to You in heaven and let me not aimlessly wander about here below. From this moment onward, You are to be my only delight; You alone are my food and my drink, my love and my joy, my sweetness and all my good.

3. Would that, by Your presence, You set me fully on fire, totally consume me, and utterly transform me into Yourself. Then, melted by love's fiery flames *I will become*, by the grace of interior union, *one spirit with You.*[1]

Do not allow me to go away from You still hungry and thirsty, but mercifully treat me as You have so often and so wonderfully dealt with Your saints. How marvelous it would be if I were wholly on fire with You, and were to dissolve away. You, Lord, are the fire that is ever burning and is never quenched;[2] You are the love that purifies the heart and gives enlightenment to the mind.

[1] 1 Cor. 6:17 [2] Cf. Augustine, *Confessions* X, 29

17. The Burning Love and Overwhelming Desire To Receive Christ

Disciple:

Lord, it is with deep reverence and burning love, with great affection and fervor of heart that I desire to receive You, just as many saints and devout persons, who were especially pleasing to You because of their holy lives and their ardent devotion, have longed to receive You in Holy Communion.

O my God, eternal Love, my only good and unending happiness, I wish to receive You with that same overwhelming longing and deepest reverence as any one of Your saints had or could have had.

2. I am, indeed, unworthy to have the same devout sentiments as Your saints; nevertheless, I offer You all the love I have in my heart, as if I alone possessed these pleasing and intense desires. Whatever a pious mind can conceive and desire, all this I present and offer to You with the greatest reverence and deepest love. I desire to keep nothing for myself, but freely and most willingly I sacrifice myself and all that I have for You.

O Lord, my God, my Creator and my Redeemer, I aspire to receive you today with the same tenderness, reverence, praise and honor, with the same gratitude, respect and love, with the same faith, hope and purity with which Your most holy mother, the glorious Virgin Mary, desired and received You when she devoutly and humbly responded to the angel that brought her the good news of the mystery of Your Incarnation: *Behold, the servant of the Lord, be it done to me according to Your word.*[1]

[1]Luke 1:38

3. And as Your blessed precursor, the most distinguished among the saints, John the Baptist, still enclosed in his mother's womb, rejoiced in Your presence and *leaped with the joy of the Holy Spirit,*[2] and later on when he discovered You walking among men, he profoundly humbled himself and with utmost love said: *The friend of the Bridegroom, who stands and hears Him, rejoices with joy at the Bridegroom's voice.*[3] So I too wish to be on fire with such great and holy desires and I desire to present myself to You with my whole heart.

Therefore, I wish to offer and present to You the jubilant joy found in all devout hearts, their burning love, their ecstasies, their supernatural illuminations and heavenly visions, together with all the virtues and praises that have been or shall ever be given You by the creatures of heaven and earth, for myself and for all who have been recommended to my prayers and that You may receive fitting praise from men and be glorified without end.

4. My Lord and my God, accept these prayers and desires of mine for Your infinite praise and immeasurable blessing; all these are rightfully Yours *according to Your exceeding greatness.*[4]

These I give You, and desire to give You each day and each moment of time, and I prayerfully and lovingly invite and ask all the spirits of heaven and all the faithful on earth to join me in offering You praise and thanksgiving.

5. Let all peoples, tribes, and tongues praise You, and, with great joy and fervent devotion, may they magnify Your most holy and sweet name. And may all who reverently and devoutly celebrate Your most august Sacrament, or receive it with the fullness of faith, deserve to find grace and mercy with

[2]Luke 1:44 [3]John 3:29 [4]Ps. 150:2

You and may they, in turn, offer a humble prayer for sinful me.

And after they shall have obtained the grace of devotion they desire, and blissful union with You, and after they have departed the holy and heavenly table, with souls warmly comforted and wondrously refreshed, may they prayerfully remember this spiritual pauper.

18. *Not Scrutinizing This Sacrament Out of Mere Curiosity but Being a Humble Imitator of Christ and Subjecting the Evidence of Our Senses to the Holy Faith*

Jesus:

You must avoid all useless prying and investigating into this most august Sacrament, if you do not want to be inundated with doubts. The man who searches into majesty will be overwhelmed by its glory!

God can accomplish more than man can ever understand. A holy and humble inquiry into truth is permissible, as long as you are prepared to be taught and are ready to walk according to the sound teachings of the Fathers.

2. Blessed is that simplicity that leaves the difficult paths of abstruse interrogation and walks along the sure and open path of God's commandments!

Many people, because they desired *to investigate what was beyond their power*[1] have lost all feeling for devotion. It is faith

[1]Sir. 3:21

and an upright life that are required of you and not a penetrating intellect nor a knowledge of the profound depths of God's mysteries.

If you neither understand nor grasp the things that are beneath you, how will you comprehend those that are above you? Submit yourself, therefore, to God and humble the evidence of your senses before faith, and you will receive the light of knowledge in the measure that is both useful and needful to you.

3. Some people undergo frightful temptations concerning the faith and this Sacrament, but these are due to the devil, and do not come from themselves.

Don't become anxious, don't enter into discussion with your thoughts, and don't try to answer the doubts that the devil suggests, but put your faith in God's words and believe His saints and His prophets, and *the wicked enemy will flee from you.*[2]

To suffer such doubts is often to the servant of God's advantage. Remember, the devil does not tempt unbelievers or sinners, for he already possesses these, but in a variety of ways he tempts and plagues those who are faithful and devout.

4. Therefore, continue in your simple but staunch faith, and approach the Sacrament with reverent humility and securely entrust to God all that you are unable to understand.

God does not deceive; but man is deceived when he places too great a trust in himself. God walks with those whose hearts are simple, He reveals Himself to those who are humble, *gives understanding to little ones,*[3] and *opens the minds of the pure,*[4] but He conceals His grace from those who are proud and yield to prying curiosity.

[2]James 4:7 [3]Ps. 119:130 [4]Luke 24:45

Human reason is weak and subject to deception; true faith, on the other hand, cannot be deceived.

5. All reasonings and natural inquiry must follow faith and not precede it nor encroach upon it. For in this most holy and most excellent Sacrament, faith and love are of utmost importance and they operate in ways unknown to man.

The eternal God, who is immense and of infinite power, does great and mysterious things in heaven and on earth, and *there is no searching out His wonderful works.*[5] If God's deeds were such that human reason could easily understand them, then they could not be properly called wonderful nor would they be beyond human description.

[5]Job 5:9

INDEX

(Roman numerals indicate Book, Arabic numerals indicate Chapter)